Dear Eric + Kelly –

How glad we are to have you here in our midst. I hope this book may be of special help to you as you let our Precious Saviour be your companion and help all the way of your life together. He is Wonderful and will be as near you as you will let Him be. So let Him be your companion every day and it will help to enrich your life in many ways. He wants to walk with you in all of your journey together. Thank you for coming and helping. In His love

Rev Marion F. Woods

A SPIRITUAL JOURNEY THROUGH POETRY WITH MARION WOODS

Marion Woods

authorHOUSE®

AuthorHouse™
1663 Liberty Drive
Bloomington, IN 47403
www.authorhouse.com
Phone: 1-800-839-8640

First published by AuthorHouse   7/1/2009

ISBN: 978-1-4389-8758-3 (sc)
ISBN: 978-1-4389-8757-6 (hc)

Printed in the United States of America
Bloomington, Indiana

This book is printed on acid-free paper.

FOREWORD

My dear husband, Marion, has just celebrated his 90th birthday of Adventure Living with his Heavenly Father.

In our preparation of this first volume of poems we have recalled many memories of people, family, friends, places, Volunteer in Mission teams, special spiritual moments and even remembered some of our adopted pets here at the Rural Center. We have lived out many of these experiences together and they have precipitated these thoughts that Marion so giftedly has captured in rhyme.

For our wedding day on April 17, 1993, Marion wrote a poem. Our daughter, Deanna Miller Clarkson, wrote the music for it and our brother, Howard S. Russell, sang the song.

These are the words of this special poem written for our special day.

TOGETHER
Together we love our Savior;
Together we sing of His fame.
Together we read the true Gospel;
Together we honor His name.

Together we follow His footsteps;
Together we serve the distressed.
Together we're touched by His miracle;
Together we've everyone blessed.

For His is the one who unites us;
And He is the one by our side.
Yes, He is the Master of the morning;
The Creator of the world so wide.

So let us everyone adore Him,
Love Him, serve Him, implore Him;
And let us tell the world about Him,
Christ Jesus, Christ Jesus, Christ Jesus,
The Lord of us all.

Marion and I are in this Adventure "Together" for as long as the Lord gives us life.
We are glad for every day of the Adventure with Him and with His people.

May this book encourage you as you read these poems to tell the world about **"Christ Jesus, the Lord of us all."**

With Him by your side, Adventure on, dear friends, more wonders are in thee!

Mary Russell Miller Woods
December 2008

INTRODUCTION

Maybe once or twice in our lives, God grants us the high honor of meeting someone special—someone who walks so closely with Christ that –for the moment—we are sure that we are walking and talking with our Savior. That is what happened when many years ago God allowed my path to cross that of Marion Woods. From that first encounter, like so many others, I knew that Marion was someone very special. His love of God, his passion and compassion for God's children were so clearly evident and contagious.

From then on, I have treasured each moment God has given us together. I urge our mission team members to "lean in close" to drink in every word Marion has to share with us. Likewise, I spend every free moment sitting as close as I can—drinking in every bit of wisdom, every ounce of inspiration and every drop of laughter.

God grants us these rare gems only so often and I thank God for the gift of Marion Woods.

Pull up a chair, sip a cup of Costa Rican coffee and be prepared to feel God's presence as Marion takes you on a walk with the Savior.

Rev. Jimmy Towson
Metter, Ga.- FUMC

My feelings about the writings and correspondence from Marion Woods go in two directions. Marion's correspondence reminds me of Paul's letters to the churches. This became especially clear to me as I use "The Message" by Eugene Peterson. On the other hand, Marion's poetry reveals his feelings related to what he sees in an instant, in a day, with a Volunteers in Mission team, with his family, or with his close friends. Marion has repeatedly awed his audience with a poem written for them or about them and captures the essence of the relationship. Marion has been prolific in his poetry and is an essential part of his daily work. The poetry is an expression of his spirituality and often his relationship to God!

"Preach the gospel at all times; if necessary use words." St. Francis of Assisi

By: Gil Hoffman

It was late on Friday night, and we were all tired from the week's work and were unloading the last team's truck. It was natural for us older men to pick up a load we could handle leaving the heavier loads for the younger men. Marion (over 80 years old) arrived and he immediately grabbed the two heaviest cans that were left on the truck.

That is an example of the way he has lived his life, always taking the heaviest physical load and always taking on the heaviest spiritual load.

By: Charles Kitchell, Abilene, TX

Marion Woods is one of the finest Christian gentlemen that the world has known, and I have had the honor of knowing him personally. My wife and I made a mission trip to his ranch in Costa Rica and what a privilege working with Marion and Mary. They weren't married at that time, but apparently Marion swept Mary off her feet as they were married shortly thereafter in Tennessee. Jean and I were honored to serve as attendants at their wedding.

We have communicated regularly for the last 12-13 years, every two months sending 900 Spanish Upper Rooms to assist with Marion's and Mary's great mission work in Costa Rica.

We are blessed to know such Godly people.

By: Gerald and Jean Lawrence, Elmore, AL

A Challenge

You who feel you are self-contained,
You who laugh at those who believe;
One day you will find yourselves deflated,
When the Lord says, "only who have faith receive."

Take all our discoveries and all your solutions,
What is there that we are not given?
Know we not, that even our minds
Have been made to wrestle and to be driven.

God's challenge to the Universe created,
Is one to seek, to work and to find.
It is to take what has been given with love;
It is to knock and to ask with the mind.

We are challenged to discover the many answers,
In a semi-hard universe we are found.
Disease, drought, earthquakes, storms and more –
Challenge us to find the answers that are bound.

We can thank God He didn't make it all easy,
Lest we become fat and die in our ease.
God has set up for us many a puzzle,
But it's for our good, with love, if you please.

So do thank Him for the world as He has made it;
Be sincere in it and get to work with a will.
Ask God for His help as you go at it rejoicing,
He's doing the working as well – just wait and stand still.

A Childhood Remembrance

What more could you ask
On a spring or summer day,
Than a lunch with a hunk of cheese,
A fishing pole and a slow moving creek –
With biting catfish, if you please.

If you can't send the fish,
Then let the crawdads come.
We'll handle them with care,
Let them get a full snapper bite,
And gently bring them through the air.

The tail of a fish isn't all that tasty;
But a crawdad's tail is juicy and sweet.
What the fish can't do with its tail,
It makes up for it with its meat.

A Drippy Roof And A Cloudy Sky

A drippy roof and a cloudy sky
Can make one start asking – why?
Why this? Why that? But also, too,
It's a good day to discover who's "you!"

Take hold of some day thought long,
Wrestle tough with good faith, strong.
Discover anew that God wants you here;
He knows your name and says it with cheer.

His love makes all the difference for sure,
Open that Good Book; find the Gospel pure.
Good news it is for you, others and me,
It helps us all know who we ought to be.

Decide to be faithful with Him whatever betide,
How much stronger we become with Him at our side.
Though the winds of misfortune be ever so strong,
He is the One who has the answers to wrong.

So little by little we are nourished and grow;
What a marvel is how He helps us to know
How great is His Father, who is our Father too.
How blessed becomes eternal life ever new.

A Jump Start

A jump start from Jesus will make you real;
It is far more than just a new way to feel.
Everything becomes real as you see with new eyes;
On every hand you meet yet another surprise.

Little children become jewels with shining faces;
Needy folk become real friends, and not just cases.
You find yourself hearing a new voice call –
It's an urgent plea to come with your all.

It promises to be with you as you go;
Behind that voice is the Person you're going to know.
He's the Living Lord Jesus – He's the Holy Spirit;
He's the Eternal Father – Creator of the Universe and what's in it.

You're invited now, so come on let's go;
Your life, too, is part of the show.
Just tumble your life now into His great hands;
He will take and show you many new lands.

He will help you to serve beyond all measure;
Your life will become more each day, a treasure.
Now you just keep on walking and following Him;
He will help you to see when lights grow dim.

For to Him the light and the darkness are all the same;
He's the Creator and it all has His stamp and name.
Just remember that life here is only part of the plan,
There is much more to your destiny than this short span.

December 20, 2005

A Little Bit of Love goes a Long Way

I thought I was in a hurry with a reason,
When by the dirty steps and wall I saw him sitting there.
Un-kept he was and under the influence for sure.
Now where was I going so fast, just where?

I felt drawn to sit down beside him to see
If there was someway I could be of help;
For, my goodness, what a state to be in!
It would be better to appear a battered lonely whelp.

We talked a little before I invited him
To go with me to get a bite to eat.
He hesitated and thought it quite impossible,
For from there, they had quite kicked out his seat.

He finally gave in to going along with me;
We probably seemed to people quite a rare pair.
It took a little special understanding from the Café owner
To let us both have a welcome there.

But as we both began to attack the food –
A good sized dish of country-style soup;
We talked and talked among his half smile and beam.
How could he, after this, really recoup?

Well, we talked about several things for sure;
We came closer to Jesus than ever before.
We felt His presence and His hand of love;
Now we could face the World aglow as we went out the door.

A Little Pessimistic

If they don't get you from one side,
They will get you from the other.
If they don't tell your father what you did,
They will whisper it to your mother.

They will borrow from you always,
And they will always promise you to pay;
But be careful how much you trust them,
Recheck what every one of them might say.

A Little Rock

I'm just a little rock,
Made by the Lord.
If you don't believe it's true,
You'll just have to take my word.

I'm just a little "heart rock"
Found in the brook;
The many years in the stream
Helped me know it like a book.

I was part of a great big boulder;
It started rolling down the hill;
The faster it rolled down the slope,
The faster it kept rolling still.

Almost down, it bounced into the air,
And crashed into the granite wall.
It split into ten thousand pieces;
I was about the littlest one of all.

I had many rugged edges to be sure,
My face was a sight to see;
But I was just glad to exist,
And to be just only me.

The many years of fine sanding,
Has helped to form my shape.
I've moved like forever, to and fro,
At times with mouth agape.

At last I took my present form,
It's in the form of a heart.
It's what I really wanted to be
From the most earliest start.

Yes, I'm a little heart rock;
God has had a hand on me.
He has used many a special manner
To make me a heart rock for others to see.

May 7, 2008

A Little Walk

A little walk with Jesus,
Even along life's weary way,
Lifts up our souls in glad belief
To keep us in tune with Him to stay.

Look there, dear ones with confidence;
He beckons us to live with joy,
When the road becomes most different,
It is then we do our faith more employ.

There is no end to our walk –
We keep on in step with Him.
Though death becomes a part of it all,
Beyond the grave we continue with more vim.

January 1, 2007
4:30 a.m.

A New Chapel for Santa Lucia

Oh yes, we need a new chapel.
The old one has served many years.
In it we've learned of our Savior,
And salvation has abolished our fears.

We've learned to become His disciples;
We experience Him daily at our side.
In the fields, the forests and the kitchen,
He's the Redeemer, Who's come to abide.

There's been enough of this talking;
It's a meaningless din in our ears.
It's time to get on with our working,
Wipe gently with love, all our tears.

We work the fields and the pastures;
We labor till the task is done.
We come to worship Him only –
All praise to the Father, to Spirit and Son.

The battle is His, the Word tells us,
After all is said and well done.
Though it seems sometimes He's hidden;
He is the difference, the battle is won!

So lift up your voices, all you people;
With one accord make known your praise.
Shout and proclaim His great miracles;
Lord of the Heavens, the Ancient of Days.

Our new chapel will be made larger
To include both the young and the old.
Though we always proclaim here the Gospel,
There is always more to be told.

We'll reach out to our friends and our neighbors;
We've a mission beyond our front door.
Farther away others still stand waiting;
We'll reach out to others more and more.

A Petal On The Walk

One early morn I took a walk
To buy a melon and a mango.
Sluggish I was, as I ambled along;
It resembled not in the least, a tango.

The fruit stands nearby were closed;
And a larger one was blocks away.
So I set out to make the longer trip,
Loosening up my joints on the way.

This pain and that ache seemed to disappear
As I took time to notice becoming flowers.
The heavens beckoned me to look their way,
Lest they send refreshing showers.

I passed the happy children;
They came by car and foot to school.
Across the street sat two red-faced rummies,
Needing to be washed in a nearby pool.

In the distance I saw the opened stand,
And quickened my step for sure;
Lo, what was that on the walk?
Yes, a hibiscus petal, beautiful and pure.

A rich, rich rose its color was;
Really was a brilliant flaming pink.
And right away there came to mind
A blessed thought, quickly as a wink.

My Heavenly Father led me this way,
Sharing with me this petal on the walk.
His love and care touched my heart,
And I found it most difficult to talk.

He gave me this lovely petal to share
With the one I dearly love.
So I put it carefully in my shirt,
And took it to my waiting turtle dove.

So now I know a secret sure,
Sealing it in my heart with a lock.
Let your Father lead you as you go,
And He'll share His beauty as you walk.

A Place to Sleep

They gave me a bed – their bed of course,
To sleep for the night and rest secure.
No mosquitoes allowed in the room at all;
Enclosed to perfection, floor, ceiling, roof and wall.

A fan to keep the temperature down,
How comfy – one of the best rooms in town!
Oh yes, there are hotels with all of the class,
But this room is given me with love amass.

At Alfredo's
Los Chiles, Costa Rica

A Touch of Wonder

A touch of wonder in the soul,
Can come at most any hour;
It may come from what we see
High in the mountains that tower.

There is real beauty in each flower,
If one has good sense to appreciate.
The Master Painter creates the dawn;
He is most ready to deviate.

The Creator has in His mind,
That which guides His every brush;
His task to reveal the Master's touch,
His joy no tender life to crush.

'Tis true, though His beauty is everywhere,
That it depends much also on the "see-er."
Some folk miss far more than they know,
The touch of wonder is also in the "be-er."

November 2006

Adventure on Man

It has been a continuation and expansion of the field of work as a
retired missionary, still active, a volunteer,
under appointment of the Bishop of the
Methodist Church in Costa Rica.

It is frosting on the cake to see and participate in the total
work of the church including the relocation of the Methodist
School, the Methodist Seminary, the founding of the University
and the development of the Methodist Rural Retreat and
Center. All this, and more intimately, in the establishing of new
congregations, the construction of churches with the tremendous
aid of the Volunteers in Mission teams – as many as three
dozen a year. It has made expansion possible from the border of
Panama to the border of Nicaragua, and invites mission efforts
beyond those borders.

Entrance into shack-town additions has opened a many faceted
effort, bringing the abundant life of the Christian faith, light and
life. This is a blessed adventure in itself.

One can do nothing but be thankful for the God given gift of a
long life that continues to expand yearly. God is good beyond our
common comprehension.

Amaryllis

Oh amaryllis, you precious lily!
Your face, a double trinity star;
There in the center, six curly spikes;
How utterly lovely you are!

Your delightful shiny features
Speak of the perfection of your Maker;
While you do regally stand there,
Of your beauty, we're everyone a taker.

Almost lost you were to us;
You, some careless soul picked,
Then let you fall to the ground
Where you, foot traffic could have kicked.

What blessings shunned people are,
When given a chance to survive.
Their lovely features burst into bloom,
Proclaiming it's great to be alive.

1995

And I Discover

Funny isn't it, my dear,
Each time I think, "It can't be true."
Just when I feel I've reached the top,
I find I'm beginning all anew.

And I discover,

New ways to address you,
New ways to show I care,
New trails on which to walk with you;
New challenges to face a dare.

Of life's cup we do drink together;
As one we work and sweat and sing.
We find there is a special joy
For us, that each new day has to bring.

Now when disaster really strikes,
Driving us into each other's arms;
'Tis there we find how much we need
Each other's warmth, each other's charms.

So my love, there is no end to it,
No last time to speak your name.
Our honeymoon is really ever new;
As each morn, love bursts into flame.

1988

Another Day

'Tis another day that's being born,
And gone is the darkest night.
Before long the sun will rise;
It will be a wondrous sight.

While hours were spent in writing down
What You'd put within my heart;
That's only a little of what You've shared –
In my soul sings the larger part.

Now I must go and rest a mite,
Then rise again to face the day.
In Thy work we're never done,
As we do it in love's own way.

"All is well," some will say
When the times demand our best.
'Tis evil's attempt to undo our faith,
And tempt us to go with the rest.

So I put myself into Your hands;
There's no better place to be.
You will guide me ever, all the way,
And help my weary eyes to see.

December 1997

As He – With Him – For Them

They come to ask for a crust;
For something to build a shelter –
It may be sheets of zinc, old or new,
Anything is better than their helter shelter.

They've never enough work to earn food
For all the mouths that seek a spoon;
What can these parents ever say,
When hunger lingers late and soon?

How tiring to the weary mothers,
Who, in spite of all they can plan and do,
It never is ever quite enough –
There should be more, even of the watery stew.

Of course, there is always more bone than meat,
Some veggies are famous for not being there,
Salt helps to bring out some of the taste,
To make the hunger be less bare.

No wonder Jesus had them sit row by row
While the disciples served the bread and fish.
He knew the difference real hunger makes,
When all one has is a desperate wish.

The self-same Jesus bids us feed
The hungry when they come to ask.
Sometimes it may be our last drip,
As into the hungry hands we cast.

Great reward shall be for all who share;
Who forget to count whatever the cost.
They have their reward in His love,
Who sought to seek and save the lost.

November 2006

At Breakfast

Here they come ready for breakfast!
Most are interested first in a coffee cup;
Really interested in what's inside,
Else they would have nothing to say.

They might get for breakfast some pinto –
That's really made of rice and beans.
To that, you can add cheese or meats;
Sometimes something more if you've means.

Of course, you would have tortillas,
Heated up or cold, but better if hot.
There might be scrambled eggs if you wish,
But don't forget to keep the coffee hot.

Another combination might be arepas –
That's the word for our pancakes.
For syrup, we use what's called dulce –
That's just cane juice boiled from sugar, for goodness sake.

We also use mile – which is our honey.
That would be served with arepas or tortillas.
With other possibilities, there comes fruit;
There's an abundance, you can bet your boots!

At My Desk

I did not intend to come here tonight;
I intended to go straight to bed.
But having to put my earphones to rest,
I've decided to stay to write, instead.

We have had a most full and precious day;
It has been filled with surprises and dreams.
Dreams that were, beforehand, almost forgotten;
Now the Lord comes closer than ever, it seems.

That He, the Creator of this, our universe,
All of it – and in it has woven His love;
That plants and trees, animals and all of us
Should display some of His beauty and love from above.

We, and all those of simple trust and faith,
Who accept His gift of life and its grandeur,
What a future awaits us in His sheer splendor,
As we establish with Him a relation of wonder.

He is most happy when He knows we love Him;
He rejoices when His care and concern do please.
It is heavenly joy when He sees us rejoicing;
He is tempted to play with us and tease.

For even God becomes a bit lonely and sad,
When one of His creation seems only as a mere sheep.
He would have us, too, to create, to copy Him;
He wishes with us a deep relationship to keep.

February 26-27, 2007

At This Late Date

At this late date in life I come;
Much done, much left to do, more to be done.
Why is it that we on grindstones put our houses?
Thinking that by our much doing, the Victory is won.

How poorly we captivate His living message:
That 'tis not nearly so much what ye do, but what ye be.
Seems like that having ears, we do not hear;
And having twenty-twenty eyes, we really do not see.

How to captivate, how to understand well?
Why do we get in our own way?
That no matter what we seem to do,
We still put the most importance on what we say.

Time begins to run out, begins to fade, vanishes;
And we are left with mouths wide open.
Our bodies weaken, wither, and rust away;
We still value most highly what is spoken.

'Tis true that we need to tell our Lord
Where we've failed, and sometimes why.
But He puts more importance on who we are;
Who we are becoming as we work, laugh, tire, and cry.

AUTUMN

The autumn leaves are always inviting me to see;
How is it that God can all at once put those colors in each tree?
Leaves of red and pink, yellow and orange, green and gold;
One tries to describe it, but only the beginning is told.

When one thinks finally it has all come together,
When it seems one can write about all kinds of weather,
When the description seems to come joyfully and free,
The morning sun streams through, and golly, gosh, oh gee!

The brilliance of the colors on every tree
Is livened up, and all the combinations are set free.
One stands or sits in awe and wonder, all agape.
Behold! The Master Designer of it all, Creator of every shade and
shape!

Written while in the United States,
November 2000

Autumn Colors, Autumn Walk, Autumn Joy

During a visit in Alabama with David and Lynda
I walked with God all over in the new, fresh, dewy morn, 1997.

I look upon a maple leaf,
To ask what hath God wrought.
Its colors captivate the eye,
To reveal the beauty sought.

I went walking in that 'Bama morn,
Sun and clouds were in the east.
School bus children waiting on the corner
Noticed my passing not the least.

The freshness of the morning air
Was strengthened by the dew.
Newly cut grass sharing its perfume
Alerted my senses, all anew.

God was speaking through His painted trees;
Autumn's flowers hailed me with joy.
Sharing the lawns with the gathered pumpkins,
There was many an abandoned toy.

The busy street with its fumes,
As the traffic came rushing by,
Hurried me to a less used lane,
Where I could see more of His sky.

Unhurried here, I walked along,
Blessed by many a joyous thought.
Residents in the houses slept;
I passed right through a vacant lot.

There awaited me, in a playground space,
Swings, a teeter-totter, and more.
But being seventy-seven (not only seven),
I only wished I'd had it all when I was four.

Over the bridge with its drainage ditch,
I crossed through still another plot.
The dewy grass fairly rinsed my feet,
Then I stopped, still on the spot.

Right there among the young maple trees –
The leaves were beginning to turn;
The reds were replacing the green tones
To make my emotions burn.

I whispered a tender apology
As I picked two of the turning leaves.
I knew the owner would understand
To say, "They are for you, if you please."

Yes, and they are for you, too, my Mary.
Like you, they are a gift of love from Him.
You color up the humdrum of life
With love's bright colors that do not dim.

Awake! Awake!

Awake, awake, my Methodist brethren!
Loyalty to Christ is more than maintenance.
If we are content only to worship sustenance,
We are left with dried up souls.

We fail to understand our Savior;
We fail to be his love slave.
Look to Him, on that cross dying,
Everything He had, He gave.

Then He sent them all to go out,
Everywhere, they all were sent.
Like Him, we are to do likewise,
Giving ourselves, before we ask for a cent.

Missionary giving demands first place,
We are asked, like Him who gave.
Everything we are and have is given,
If we are the world to save.

Following in the footsteps of our Master,
We walk the roads of the world.
Even the lonely sacrifice walk,
As Eternal Love's Story is told.

Rise up, O church of Christ!
You dare not lose your soul.
Your missionary task is first of all,
Lest you at last, lose the whole.

Centro Rural Metodista, July 13

Banana

I'm a little banana and my coat is green;
On the other hand I'm white inside – but that's unseen.
Sometime in the future I'm going to be yellow;
When that day comes to pass, I'll be sweet and mellow.
I don't know who it is that's going to eat me;
I guess it doesn't matter much, 'cause then I'll cease to be.

December 15, 2005

Be Like the Lily

Be like the lily in all of its splendor;
Let shine all that God has put within you.
Turn your life over to His gracious love;
You will discover His presence in all that you do.

All He needs in our lives is real recognition;
Permission to make our whole heart His throne.
Our actions then become His deeds, done through us all;
We're made able to do His will, and His will alone.

Oh, the rich feeling of being at peace with our God;
Of knowing that in Him we're really made whole.
Fears fall away and doubts cease to be;
Through obedience to Him, we meet our life's goal.

No words will ever sound sweeter to our ears
Than His words at last, when the victory is won.
These are the words He's promised us, you know –
They are the words, "My daughter, my son, well done, well done."

June 8, 1997

Be Still, He is Speaking

Be still, He is speaking;
Though there be no special sound.
His presence you can feel,
And you stand on Holy Ground.

As He has promised,
He is only a thought away.
He has come, but He is always here.
Hark! It's time to wait and pray.

Open yourself to God and be
Forever able to be in tune.
You'll find Him coming, and also here –
No matter be it morning, night or noon.

Be Ye Therefore Perfect

What is it that I must tell you,
Before I must look for my bed;
What is it that is in my heart,
And will not stay out of my head?

It is the conviction that we need more
Courage to state our convictions every day.
The faith we have must be declared,
Moreover it must be lived, to show the way.

It is easy at times to use big words,
To copy the ideas of others without weighing.
It, however, satisfies the depths of us more
When we know that we're living what we are saying.

The Gospel of Jesus as God's only Son,
Who came to save all of us on earth;
When believed with all the heart and soul;
It ends in our having a real rebirth.

All things will seem to be new to us,
Because we see them with new eyes.
The eyes of faith see from the best;
They change our thinking and being beyond surprise.

New thinking about our Heavenly Father grows;
We see His love for us in His Son.
It speaks to all – who we are and can become;
We know this new life will never be undone.

We believe we shall go on from victory to victory.
Jesus invited us to be perfect, as God the Father is.
Eternal life begins now in this life, and keeps growing;
What joy fills our lives as we make being like Him our biz.

November 17, 2007

Before Retiring

I know that I shall never find
Love like His, so gracious and kind.

But it shall be recognized, my friend,
If you will let Him, your heart attend.

All He needs is a crack in your door,
He will come right in and bless you more.

Give Him that chance and treat Him well,
He'll fill your heart and ring your bell.

The sound will awaken others to sing;
Helping them the good tidings, also, to bring.

Then you shall be able to sleep,
And rest real well without counting sheep

Goodnight.

June 7, 2004

Better Do It

Many things seem to say good-bye
As I go passing them by.
Do you suppose they know more;
More about my future history than I?

It seems to be too much of a bother,
Too much to lock everything up tight.
Could it be that they are warning me
About what's going to happen in the night?

I rather think, though, its something else;
It's God's alarm clock built within us.
Some people may call it mere intuition,
But God's love seeks to keep us from a lot of fuss.

So I'll keep locking things up when He whispers;
Just reminding me always to be a little careful,
Because things just seem to vanish if you don't –
It's then you sit down and are tearful.

Yes, you had better do it or you'll be sorry,
Yes, you will be sorry if you don't.
The tearful ones among the multitude
Are the ones who have said, "I won't."

So, I locked the second door of my car just in case.
Thank you Father!

November 26, 2007
(Before breakfast after taking folks to school.)
Note: 6 months later, they poisoned and killed a half dozen dogs,
and robbed heavily our tools and equipment. Now we have guard
every night.

Between God and Man, No Strife!

But why shouldn't it happen this way?
God is in control, and in His time,
He's ready to bring in, as He will,
His great Salvation for all, sublime.

For you and me, it seems a bit rare,
He comes in the form of the lowliest low,
That the highest of the High might reveal Himself,
In a love that all can know.

This love is one that's beyond all else;
It's from the heart of the Creator of all life.
There is none else that can be so great,
Ending between God and man, the meaningless strife.

December 1997

Bread and Water and Jesus, Too!

Bread and water and Jesus, too!
God offers, daily, the same for me and you.
We may not have a lot to eat,
But, oh, the fellowship is sweet!
What we do have becomes a feast;
The Love of Jesus is for the least.
His presence is enough for us;
We get along without the fuss.
Many other things call at the gate,
But right now those things can wait.
When we take time to be with Him,
The importance of some things grows dim.
He makes the difference in our life;
Peace begins to reign amid the strife.
Help comes to us from above;
We see much clearer with eyes of love.
God is real and long His reach;
Those high barriers He does breach.
He sets aflame the open heart;
He promises to stay, and not depart.
So just now let us welcome Him;
Receive His love, the power and the vim!
Then we will be ready for His call
To go and spread His Gospel – Go to all!

March 11, 2002
(Six months after The Towers)

Breakfast Time

The sun is up and I hear the pup
A hollerin' for his morning food.
If I don't get there within a hair,
I'll have to feed all of the brood.

Because, you see, I'm not free;
Their mother was killed by a car.
How many times each day they whine and say,
"It's time you bring our food jar."

May 8, 2008

Brothers In Him

In the middle of the night
While the stars were shining bright,
God's amazing love came down
O'er the countryside and town.

Knowing what is in His word,
Angelic voices, too, were heard.
God is speaking to each heart,
Offering blessings from the start.

Whosoever will may come,
Joyous faith in God at home.
Forgiveness floods forever sweet;
Shepherds falling prostrate at His feet.

Glorious salvation for one and all –
List oh list, to His tender call.
As you believe by faith, and come,
He fills your heart, and then some.

Now I, too, am so glad that Jesus found me;
Forgave my sins and set me free.
My cup is filled to overflowing –
Now I know where I am going.

I am so glad that Him I can see,
Really can see, really Him I can see.
By faith I believe, and Him I can see.
I am so glad that Jesus found me.

I must tell others that in Him we are brothers,
In Him we are brothers, in Him we are brothers,
I must tell others that we are brothers,
As we all have faith in Him.

But Jesus

Life seems far too short,
One always wants more and more;
This is true for me, you see,
Even when finishing eighty-four.

No one ever really knows,
When the finger at Heaven's door,
Will beckon with a "come here" sign,
Then of life <u>here</u>, there is no more.

Yet there are still others
Who know life as a chore;
Suffering and even disappointment
Makes them utter a sad "no more."

But Jesus came to assure us,
"The best is yet to come,"
This earthly life is but a preparation
To live with God, in His vast home.

August 31, 2007

Christian Love Makes A Difference

Christian love makes all the difference in the world; Christian love makes all the world different. Christians help you discover Love Eternal, the One who is the source of all love, life, goodness, and beauty. In Him, with Him and through Him all becomes to us beautiful. Through His redemptive power, His loving grace, His touch, and His being we see His love. To Him all is beautiful, all is His, as it is. He loves it all in His will. He never runs out of options; He cannot be outdone; He cannot be changed. He is always and forever Love. It will all eventually find Him, so go ahead and give in to His beautiful loving will. Thus all will be on the road to more wonderful, greater things in life, because of our Eternal God of love. He alone overcomes all that hurts and destroys; even the evil in each generation, person, and thing that is. His love accepts it even as His Son accepted it and endured the cross, despising the shame and rising above it. Therefore His love is beyond it, in it, on it, and by it we are shown Life, Resurrection! Eternal everlasting life is given, eternal love overcomes all things and includes all in His masterpiece. The mill of God grinds majestically and exceedingly fine for it is by, with, and for His love that it grinds. Suffering all pain, all shame, all hurt, all revenge, and all ugliness become transformed. Our Maker loves us and will not let evil have the last word. With Him, it is Love, Life, and Eternal Beauty.

Come Along

Come on now, come, come along;
Come let your life be a new song.

Just open up now your big heart,
Come know Jesus, and get a new start.

He will help you be a real friend;
Enjoying Holy love, and a new trend.

Sins depression cripples no more,
Freedom's joy comes in to restore.

Leap up and ride on the King's Highway;
You're sitting right beside Him, and with Him to stay,

You're in it to win it with Him;
Let that life of yours take on new vim.

Reach out and take the hand of another,
She or he will become your sister or brother.

United in Christ, overcoming defeat;
You will be a blessing to all you meet.

God's really calling you right now,
Say yes to Him, and He'll show you how.

Just like Jesus, be His servant too,
Serve Him to the end and be true.

God takes on from there after death;
Eternal life is real, man can take a new breath.

December 20

Come and Go

And so I said to this new day,
"What can I do to make things work right?"
I'll have to do more than sit and pray;
I'll enter with the Lord into the fight.

Whoever doesn't believe that God's alive,
Had better take a second look to see;
How He calls forth His own who strive
To conquer evil, and to set men free.

Set free from their much lesser selves,
Made in His image, desiring the best,
They'll not be content to be mere elves;
They'll be working giants among the rest.

God's own men, daring to take a stand;
Facing evil in the eye wherever found;
They make life worth living throughout the land;
Honest men with Christian principles, true and sound.

Come, ye men, rise up and serve the Lord!
Set the pattern for all of life!
You follow One who ever keeps His word,
And gives His all to defeat meaningless strife.

Free you are, yet bound, like Him to be –
Servant, friend, true blue to the end;
Tearing away evil's blindness, opening eyes to see.
You, too, are God's chosen whom He does send!

Go out! Out to the highways and byways to tread!
Multitudes await your coming over here and there.
They're tired and hungry; they need to be fed.
Take His welcome, "Come to the feast!" Go! Go everywhere!

Creation Continues

Last night You were my teacher,
As the sun sank in the West;
You gave me a great blessing,
As You put Your world to rest.

Yonder on the western skyline
Stood Volcano Arenal as a perfect cone;
Deep, dark blue was its fair form,
While all around the setting sun shone.

That brilliant ball struck the clouds
To create many a brilliant hue;
As I drove along in my Toyota
Every turn brought something new.

The more I drove and the more I looked,
A new thought came clearly to me;
Any painting made of Arenal's sunset
Would be as real as real can be.

"Tis true because it's ever changing,
With clouds and sky, sun and horizon fair;
God paints a new picture every minute;
You can paint it as you care.

He knows no limitations, no chains;
He's ever creating this, His world.
His options are limitless forever,
He's at it with flags unfurled.

August 26, 1996

Dearest One

Dearest one, you are always lovely, you're resting.
The day is done and night has turned again to morn.
Having collapsed into that lovely waiting bed,
I slept, renewing this old body, tired and worn.

Now this famous, burdened, rounded table,
Almost never free of work left undone,
Welcomed me to share again my energies;
To put things in order before I leave on the run.

Why is it that sometimes it seems
The more you do, the more there still remains?
There is no end to that endless line;
The routine has you bound with chains.

And yet that really is the price of being here;
It's part of life to have more than you can ever do.
It helps if you can, as you labor each day,
Meet everything with a will that's fresh and new.

Determination is a good word if practiced daily;
It keeps our eyes upon the task and load.
It helps us see what's being accomplished
And pushes us further down the road.

And when we're called to lay down the tools,
Whether they be of iron or of software,
We can have a sense of satisfaction,
Having worked hard, rejoicing in tender, loving care.

July 16, 1997

Fences

Fences are made to keep people out,
Fences are made to keep others in,
The "outs" just stand at the fence and shout,
The "ins" ask to go where they have never been.

The "ins" and the "outs" are found in us all,
We've wanted out, or in, whatever the day,
We too have stood there continuing to call,
In spite of what we hear others say.

2007

Gardening

Where, oh where did the little seeds go?
I can't find them anywhere.
They've turned into big bushes, lad,
Just look over here and there.

Now soon will come the blossoms;
They'll dance and sing in the breeze.
Then they'll turn into little tomatoes,
You can pick the first one, if you please.

Later on we'll save some seeds
And plant them in boxes early next spring.
They'll soon be ready for transplanting;
Now isn't gardening a wonderful thing?

It doesn't end with just the work;
The harvest is a great big joy.
We make juice and relish, and preserves too;
Sliced tomatoes, catsup, spaghetti sauce – oh boy!

2004

Gentle Breezes

The gentle breezes of God keep flowing
O'er all the vast countryside,
To refresh the morning workers ,
And bless them all, whate'er betide.

They make no distinction as they bless
The many lives as they touch;
Just moving along with hardly a breath,
But oh, they help so very much!

When they don't blow, when all grows still,
When leaves cease to dance,
'Tis then they are missed by everyone
Whose life they can enhance.

That's when our hearts turn more to God;
With eyes wide open we stop to pray.
We thank Him for His gentle winds
And His blessings that come each day.

Blow on, gentle breezes, do blow on;
How precious is your every kiss!
We thank our Lord for sending you
Who never leave us alone nor amiss.

September 14, 2000

Getting Older

I'm on the move for sure,
Leakingly, in a hurry, to the stool.
On other days, it was not thus;
I left then not even one tiny pool.

But things are different now;
Some of the bushings are most worn.
Or is it less resilient muscles
That cannot hold back in early morn?

That's just part of life, I guess.
Like worn out autos we bump along,
Seldom getting anywhere on time,
Yet we are glad we still belong.

Each little blessing is more real;
Time slips by and day is done.
No going back to make changes,
We press on till the victory's won.

This body slowly wastes away;
We may see changes day by day,
But our eyes are on Jesus, our Lord;
His love keeps us on the way.

Each night finds us with less time
To do what we would through Him.
His precious presence aids us so much
As we silently dominate each whim.

Getting Ready

We are privileged to share in worship.
There is singing, sharing, preaching, and prayer.
There is time to open our hearts and souls
Before we go to witness, both here and there.

The "getting-ready" spirit soon is in gear.
So many sounds for one to hear.
Some are already packed up well;
Others are at it, most pell mell.

Though there is still more work left to do,
Before we turn away no longer face to face,
It's time to climb aboard the bus and the plane.
We go back home to give witness in our daily place.

We will not soon forget what we've done,
As we've come to this fair land.
We've more reason to put love in action
And for Jesus, always, to take our stand.

February 11, 2006

Getting to Other Things

And so I must get to other things,
Like straightening up this desk and table.
There are letters to be formed and sent;
Plans await to be made, as I am able.

But I must take it all to Him,
There must be prayer and waiting;
No plans are sufficiently made,
Without His Kingdom's love and rating.

February 2004

"GO"

Let them run!
Let them walk!
If they get there,
Let them talk.

Who'd ever thought
They'd ask for a car!
Let them hitch-hike,
It ain't far.

They're the ones
Who've heard the "GO!"
Let them prove it
If it's so.

We'll stay back
And watch and wait,
We're the keepers
Of the gate.

If they get there
To preach and tell,
Then is when
We'll wish 'em well.

But never give 'em
All they ask.
Keep 'em humble
In their task.

Keep them poor!
Keep them humble!
Cut their pay
If they grumble.
And cut it more if they mumble!

April 1987,
Written after our conversation about Missionaries

Go Ye

One more ocean to sail,
One more sky to fly,
One more country to visit,
One more field to try.

Go ye into the whole world,
Go ye, and don't look back,
He promises always to be with you,
And to help with whatever you lack.

Praise Him, praise Him, praise Him,
He goes before you today,
Tumble yourself into His keeping,
He loves you and knows all the way.

God At Work In Us

Oh, you who must have the latest,
You who have sold out to style.
There is beauty that bursts forth;
It is His doing within us all the while.

God is at work within you, if you will;
You are made to live and to glorify His name.
It is His great love at work within you;
His redeeming love will not let you remain the same.

There is no limit to what you can do and be;
With Him all things are possible for sure.
His promises are not empty words;
They become reality, lovely, real, and pure.

You are created by the Creator, you see;
Your beauteous glory is found in Him.
It comes not nearly so much by self-effort,
As allowing the Creator to work in you, without whim.

He is our light, our life, our love, our all in all;
It is He who knows what's always best for us.
Being at one with Him opens the doors
Of grace and mercy in us, without all that fuss.

So, Lord, here is this heart and life for You;
We bow before You, obedient to Your will.
We know You will do all You are allowed to do
As we live before You with a spirit yielded and still.

God Is

God may be a consuming fire,
But he is also an overflowing heart.
Of His commandments men may tire,
But from His love once known, they care not depart.

Think ye that you can exhaust that love?
No! Eternal is its source, its flame.
Though centuries and eras come and go,
Our Eternal God of love is ever the same.

On a cross of shame He died for us;
He rose again to lead us ever on.
Both you and I are called to share
To give witness that His kingdom come.

November 10, 2007

God's Wonders

Dancing like leaves in a whirlwind,
Blown about by the swirling currents,
Surprisingly anxious to find their kind
Whipping about on tiptoe amid the torrents.

Storms both make new friends and leave others waiting,
Decisions are made instantly and moment to moment.
It's time to forget about all the hating,
Persons become important regardless of race, color, or raiment.

Life and goods are to be protected and saved,
Sacrifices are made, really great spirits are born,
New ways for cooperation appear, new roads are paved,
And some things become discarded, their time 'most outworn.

Yet spontaneously the little leaves are called to dance
Lightly along with seeds that barely touch the ground.
It matters not the music, they still whirl and prance,
They seem to have been a whirlwind from springs unbound.

Be ready, ye who claim to live by the Spirit's leading,
Have in you the incarnate Spirit of His Gentle Lord;
That when the storms come, you hear His pleading
And thus find yourself dancing by direction from above.

2005

Gotta Learn To Do Better

I'm tired of this silly mess;
Sore throat, sneezing, burning eyes,
Salt water gargling, surges of heat.
It's about time I started getting "wise."

Couldn't expect to improve all at once,
But after all these years of getting old
You would think I would be wiser;
After all that my mother has me told.

Next time I see the hospital sign
"Winter is coming, get your flu shot now,"
I bet I'll get Mary and Papa, and go.
We'll get in that line of oldsters – and how!

Then there will be much less of this –
This everlasting coughing, sneezing, and fever,
Surges of heat and feeling faint,
Gasping for breath and fightin' for cover.

Then sweatin' it out in the night,
First not enough blankets, then too many,
Racing to the bathroom with one foot bare,
Tripping on the throw rug, 'taint that funny.

Talkin' about "oldsters" – I'm that now;
Why, I'm already one that's eighty-eight.
I've got to get to doin' quick some learnin'
Or 'fore I know it, it's gonna be too late!

Lord of life, help me now, please.
Train that pea brain you me gave,
So I do some things much better
Than those ancestors of mine, who lived in a cave.

May 6, 2007

He Calls, We Answer

And can it be that God will reveal
To us mortal men His Holy Will?
Yes my friend, the self same God
Keeps His every promise still.

How shall it be that we shall walk
In His Kingdom's straight and narrow way?
It shall be with our joyous faith,
By His grace on that road we stay.

When shall it be that we're called of God,
Our precious pact with Him to keep?
It's right when we meet Him face to face,
And vow to help Him His harvest reap.

Where shall it be that we shall go
To make known His Gospel's saving power?
It's to everywhere throughout the earth
We go to share each day and hour.

With whom shall it be that we will march
In cadence through the rest of life?
To witness to so great a love
That keeps life radiant in midst of strife?

No matter how or when or where;
Still we're called by Him to go.
We know for sure beyond all doubt,
We must go together to help others know.

Then when we've served and daily loved,
When at last the victory's won,
We shall hear His tender voice
Whispering, "Well done, my child, well done".

Yes it's God's will, all this and more;
For He is Lord of all the earth.
And it's been known since time began,
Long before Christ's marvelous birth.

2003

He Is Here

Look, the Lord is nigh,
Come from far up high,
In the Spirit He speaks,
Listen, 'tis you He seeks.

He calls us all to His table,
Even those who are unable;
It's an invitation to His feast!
All are invited, even the least.

He, our Savior, to us calls,
Down each street and by the century walls.
May we be faithful in our task.
Whatever is that? You may ask.

It is the same as all have been told,
"Go ye into all the whole wide world,
Tell them all of Him, the God of love,
He is not imprisoned in Heaven above."

He lives and moves and is right here,
Listen to His words of good cheer.
"I am with you always" I am there,
I died to save you all, see how I care.

Let us day by day be on the go,
Showing how He does love us so,
Awake to every kind of need,
Ever sowing and planting His precious seed.

In due time His harvest does come,
Come join me now, let's share some.
"Come take some and learn of me.
Let yourself be fertile ground."

August 21, 2007

He's the One

With Jesus the Victory is always sure.
Without Him we lose our way.
I'll follow Him, my Savior, true,
No matter what others' may say.

They may laugh and scorn and shout,
You're following a vacant dream!
I'll show them what real life's about
Thru the touch of Him who does redeem.

It's really quite amazingly simple;
You just let God be who He claims to be.
It's trusting His great love shown through Jesus
And letting His spirit renew you and me.

January 2008

His Canvass

And so you see, my good friend,
If God thinks of the tiniest little tree,
And He considers the tiniest little tree frog,
He takes notice, much more, of you and me.

He is God Almighty, Creator, Father God.
He doesn't hide His beauty here and there;
The whole world is His canvass huge
And He spreads, like paint, His beauty everywhere.

His touch creates for us both rhyme and reason
In whatever the moment calls for Him to do.
He just is His wonderful, awesome, marvelous Self;
And many times His ways are beyond me and you.

But the more we live and think and try
To follow in the way His Son has done,
The more we understand His awesome nature
And seek to unite with Him as one.

"My Father and I are one," Jesus told them.
He wants to be your Father, too.
Life with Him can become so marvelous
That you feel at home with all being ever new.

September 4, 1994

His Gentle Call

I opened my heart and the Spirit came in,
He cleansed my being without and within.
The burning fire purified my soul,
His love forgave me and made me whole.

Now I can sing among all the rest,
Those who have been freed and blest.
New meaning comes in a full new life,
Victory rejoices in growth over strife.

Each morning offers a new song fest,
Followed by prayer with soul rest.
Prepared for facing each new day,
Thankful to Jesus for life's new way.

His presence is more than fine gold,
Makes real the greatest story every told.
Come my brother, my sister, my all,
Let us wait for Him and His gentle call.

Chorus:
"Go" He says, go tell one, tell all,
Help them rise up when they fall.
Take them firmly by the hand,
Help them walk, help them stand. (Repeat)

August 12, 2003

His Showers Come

Did I hear a drip drop –
A drip, drip, drop?
Yes, look, here they come, a whole sky full;
A sky full of dripping drops.
Full they are to overflowing,
Some of them unite
To become overflowing drops
Racing to the earth they come,
To dampen, to wet, to soak the earth
That there be life.
Sent they are with the Maker's love,
Messengers of growth from above.
For there shall be showers of blessing,
Showers of blessing from above.

May 2007

Homegrown on Our Plot

I took a drink of pineapple juice.
Oh, I tell you, it hit the spot!
One reason why it tastes so good
Is that it's homegrown on our plot.

We were beginners at the game
When we first planted it last year.
Yes, we made mistakes right in stride,
But worked without a fear.

You have to believe that you can,
And put your shoulder to the task.
If you don't know how to do some part,
Why, it doesn't hurt to up and ask.

There's no need to show our ugly pride
Making others feel less than good.
We are here to help our neighbor first;
To learn from them, if we just would.

May 16, 1997

Written after tasting pineapple juice Mary made from our first
pineapples produced at the Rural Center in San Carlos, Costa Rica

How Bright

How bright the light for my eyes;|
Laser-operated, they give surprise.
There is need for a cap to stop the glare,
Even from the fluorescent light up there.

How fortunate can one person be,
Given anew the blessing to see?
No more reason to guess what's written;
It all fits well, like a soft mitten.

Thank you again, God of our lives,
For your blessings daily and every surprise.
You are far greater than my imagination,
Lord of Glory, Creator of all creation.

So tonight I would praise Thee
For making Thy world – all that be.
Then what a blessing, best of all,
You keep us, hold us, not letting us fall.

Thy love captivates us, yes all of us –
All who would trust Thee without a fuss;
Join Thee in the adventure of eternal life
Gone forever the sufferings of this world's strife.

July 17, 2007

I Am – I Be

I be in You who I am,
You have made me be,
Thy work, Great Three in One,
Has made me one in Thee.

By Thy Son thy work was done,
Nailed there to that tree;
The victory for all was won,
From sin you set all free.

For shame if we do not see,
What cost we have been to Thee,
Thus on bended knees we bow,
We come to ask Thee now.

Thy forgiveness from the heart,
That we begin a truly new start,
With no ending on this earth,
Nor loss of eternal worth.

June 2, 2007
1:15 AM

If I Should Die

If I should die in the morning,
I'll be glad to see the sunrise.
To have heard the birds' morning chorus,
And have seen God's beauteous surprise.

He shares His marvelous creation,
Always revealing something that's new,
There's more to His infinite universe,
No matter what we've seen or knew.

If I should die at noontime,
When the sun is high overhead,
I'd like it to be beneath a shade tree,
Or with a fresh breeze blowing 'cross my bed.

It would be fun to have worked all the morning,
To have earned the right for some rest,
Like Jesus, we'd have worked with the Father,
And put to use our talents with zest.

If I should die in the evening,
I'd like it to be facing the West.
There to see His colors – all glorious;
Master painter is He – the best.

If I should die at Midnight,
When most of the world is asleep,
I'd just go on to be with Jesus;
For, you see, there's no need to weep.

No matter whenever He calls me,
It'll be a call at last to come home.
The door will be there wide open;
No more need to search or to roam.

Oh, He is the Lord of the Morning,
And He's also the keeper of the night;
He stands there at the doorway –
Heaven, Living Lord, what a sight!

2007

I'm Most Grateful

Oh dear Lord, I'm most grateful
For all these years you've given me.
Just think what I'm to be thankful for,
I've had eighty-eight years, and not sixty-three.

My memory now fails on every side;
It just forgets the most common of things.
But oh, the joy of what I can remember,
What a satisfaction and peace it brings.

After all, if a person could remember everything
And talk about it all the live long day,
One would be chatting like a magpie or parrot,
And people would care less what he had to say.

So, "grow old along with me," the poet said,
Why sure, "the best is yet to come."
We can appreciate more the love of God
As we draw nearer to our eternal home.

March 18, 2007

I'm With You

The horizons were closed in all around,
Except for that glorious window in the west.
God's setting sun colored the sky,
With shades of red at their best.

The shafts of light in streaming rays,
Were pronounced against the reddened sky,
They seemed to be an entrance way
Into the heavens as the day bid all good bye.

There come to me most deep emotions,
As God pictured His entrance into the night.
He seemed to be showing me a prelude
Of the time of my entry into His marvelous light.

Nor star, nor moon were seen as yet,
God seemed to be saying "come unto me,"
Let us dwell and reason together,
In mutual love and grace most free.

Pausing on the road to take it all in,
Thanksgiving flowed from my grateful lips.
He whispered, :I am with you always as you go,
I'm with you always on all your trips."

Such assurance now makes each day
A new experience with Him on my walk,
Whether by car, by plane or a foot,
His presence means more confidence as I talk.

His great Good News dances ready in my heart
Wherever His calling leads me on the way,
Nothing is there that prepared me more,
Than to know that He is with me to stay.

March 13, 2008

In the Evening

The dentists will fill and pull out your teeth,
Pull out your teeth, pull out your teeth,
They'll make your smile like a Christmas wreath,
And you'll sing a new song in the evening.

The physiotherapist will ease your pain,
Will ease your pain, will ease your pain,
You'll even be able to skip again,
And you'll dance as you sing in the evening.

The nurse will say "yes" and oh and ahhhh,
And oh and ahhhh, and oh and ahhhh,
She'll be your best friend – after your "Ma,"
She'll sing by your side in the evening.

When it's time for all to go to sleep,
To go to sleep, to go to sleep,
There's always someone who counts his sheep,
Else he'd keep singing beyond the evening.

Mary placed Jesus in a manger low,
In a manger low, in a manger low,
Shepherds said, "Well, what do you know?"
And the angels sang that evening.

There is a call for you to sing,
For you to sing, for you to sing,
You, too, can help the good news to bring,
So sing it with joy in the evening!

December 29, 1998

Indian Blood in My Veins

The other day I heard someone say
That some of my folks were quite sad
Because there is some Indian blood
Flowing in the veins we got from Mom and Dad.

But somehow I feel very proud
That I'm part Indian in my being.
I feel it in my love of creation
And in my hearing, as in my seeing.

Skies and clouds way up there,
Or flowers and birds right near here;
The wide vast seas and mountains high,
Sun, moon, and stars all bring good cheer.

At one, at one, I really feel
With the world and it's awesome Maker.
Amazed I stand and I'm so filled,
Ashamed for being just a taker.

So, here I am, Lord, do what you will;
Take me, use me, speak through me.
I am Thine, carrying in my veins Indian blood,
Ready to help make known your sweet liberty.

November 1997
(After a visit to Brother Raymond)

Jesus is Lord and Savior

Yes, there are days when one is tempted
To throw in the towel and quit;
Though it is not against the Lord
That one is throwing a fit!

It is rather a protest against evil;
Evil, in general, always messing things up.
We will stay loyal in the battle,
We will drink the entire cup.

Though it be one of suffering and shame,
With Him we will see it trough.
We share with Him the will of redemption,
We will walk the Via Dolorosa too.

We trust the end is in His hands
And He is in the hands of God, the Father.
We know that however great the cost,
Like Him there is none other.

So right on, Jesus Lord, our Savior,
We dare to follow as You lead.
We are in Your hands on the road;
You fulfill our every need.

July 2007

Let Me See

Let me see the Man who healed me;
Whisper in my ear His name.
Since He touched me and smiled,
I will never again be the same.

So many years all racked with pain,
Never able to work or play with the rest.
He has opened to me a new world;
I'm His name I must be at my best.

Others must know there is relief;
That they need not suffer all alone.
In a moment His tender healing touch
Makes whole: spirit, mind, body, and bone.

Have you heard of Him or seen Him?
They say He's come from yonder Galilee.
My friend, if you ever see Him,
Give Him my gratitude; tell Him, please, for me.

They say He has love enough for every one;
No one need be left without His cure.
He is generous with His compassion;
His gracious salvation is forever sure.

Let me see the One who healed me;
I must bow prostrate at His feet.
My heart and soul wish to praise Him,
How I long, again, Him to meet.

May 13, 2002

Letting God Control

The rain has me in the car,
Hoping that it will quit.
Once I can get out to work,
I will work until I quit!

Delays all day have come along
To change hourly my every plan.
But I have let the Lord take over,
Following Him, to do what I can.

I've found it works out best
As God takes over the day.
If I just quit trying to control,
God soon reveals a better way.

Some folk sorta laugh at that,
But they're still coming in late.
My work has long been finished
As they come ambling through the gate.

May 10, 2007

Linger a Little Longer

Linger a little longer, don't just get up and go,
He may be getting you ready for more than you ever know,
Yes, linger a little longer, that too is a part of prayer,
Practicing His Holy presence, you'll find He's always there.

He's there right beside you, He's nearer than hands and feet.
You may need to get a going, but wait a bit to leave your seat.
Listen to His wise counsel, sense His loving sharing power,
It will help you be victorious throughout each passing hour.

Take time to really listen, let Him have His word with you;
Linger for His preparation for all you'll go and do.
This in-depth time is needed before the day has yet begun,
It helps you know He's with you, when you're really on the run.

Linger a little longer, linger though it yet be night,
Jesus did that very thing before He loved with all His might.
Those extra moments with His Father, prepared Him very well,
The Good News was always fresh news, as He went out to tell.

Thank you, Lord, for lingering and teaching us to do the same,
Before we go share the Gospel, help us wait to praise your name;
Then when we meet the problems, be them of others or our own,
We meet them with His power, for we battle not alone.

Linger a little longer, linger on and on and on,
Meet and praise the Holy Spirit, the Father and the Son,
Oh linger a little longer, linger on and on and on,
Meet and praise the Holy Spirit, the Father and the Son.

Then go empowered by Him and Them,
You go with the Holy Three in One,
They make you able, free and full,
You will battle evil till the victory is won.

Little Cloud

I saw a little cloud
Floating up in the air.
After I said hello to my kitty,
That little cloud wasn't there.

I looked and looked around,
Saying, this isn't fair.
I can't see it anymore,
Hiding up in thin air.

Maybe I could talk to it,
For playing hide and seek;
Maybe it could teach me
How better I should peek.

That way I could look around
Most any kind of corner;
Without being seen a bit
And ending up a goner.

June 2007

Long-Stemmed

One tall flower in a tall vase
Barely has room left to show its face;
Gracing the table there in the center,
Says "hi" to us all as we enter.

It is a beautiful red color, every petal;
Watching by its side the warm tea kettle.
It even stands out more when it's alone;
There it shines with its special tone.

It whispers that its there for you to see,
So you can thank God for all that be.
Aren't flowers good friends, every one,
Greeting us always till day is done?

August 2007

Look

It's a new day! What will I do with it?
It's the gift of God for today, right there given.
It's all wrapped up in a great big beautiful world;
Beauty is everywhere, enormously wrapped even.

This wrapping cover bounces around all day everywhere;
Yes, and the colors are there all over the place.
There are little creatures racing around at work and play;
They are able to do thousands of things with real grace.

You know I took time to look in a mirror,
And there I found a creature that was really rare.
He's not all that handsome, with those tired eyes and face,
And it doesn't help his looks at all, that long white hair.

If I were he, I would get me another looking glass;
Even making it my first purchase today at a store.
Maybe I could find it in one of the many big superstores,
A looking glass with a handle that would my looks restore.

If that doesn't work, maybe his wife could help,
So she won't have to put up with that sight.
They might have somewhere, some very special glasses,
Some that she can wear and take away all the fright.

If that is impossible, maybe you could at least cut his hair.
You would have to do it, however, when he is asleep.
Oh my! Maybe that isn't such a good idea after all –
For how then could he his Santa Claus appointments keep?

November 21, 2007

Look and See

Look ye there with sound of trumpet,
Gabriel, sent of God on this day,
Calling us out of sleepy dreamland
To accept His presence as we pray.

Open wide those seeing wonders!
What splendid cameras both of them are,
Created to see the wonders of the world;
Able to examine all, both near and far

Today our eyes can be repaired;
Cataracts are laser-ed off each day.
What wondrous new sight is revealed;
All colors are brighter, new sight to stay.

I kneel in gratitude and wonder
At what great a gift He has given me!
Letting me, who saw all things blurred,
Now am able His great world to see.

Praise to your Name, Marvelous Father,
Tender beyond all your mighty display.
May I never fail to thank you
For your beauties revealed by night and day.

November 3, 2006

Lord Jesus

Lord of the morning,
Keeper of the night,
Help us to remember
You're the giver of light.

Even the Light of the World
Is Jesus, God's only Son.
He said so His own self;
By Him life's victories are won.

Midnight on August 31, 2003

Lord, We Have Come

Lord, we've come to the mission field,
We've come to help with the yield,
We've come with the Gospel of cheer,
We found You already here.

Here Your name is also glorified,
Many hearts come, opened wide;
You fill them with Your gracious power,
While they praise you by the hour.

Oh yes, You're at work on the field,
You are bringing in an abundant yield,
More people have a new heart,
Now they are more ready to do their part.

There shall be no end to this,
It ever leads to eternal bliss.
Thus we come and go in His name,
Costa Rica will not be the same.

Where You are loved and served,
The spirit of the faithful is ever daily.
There is joy each day in heart and soul,
It is fruit of those by You made whole.

We sing glory, glory to Your name,
We're so glad to work, we came.
Oh glory, glory to your gracious name,
We will never be the same.

2002

Love In Action

We are privileged to share in worship.
There is singing, sharing, preaching, and prayer.
There is time to open our hearts and souls
Before we go to witness both here and there.

The "getting-ready" spirit soon is in gear.
So many sounds for one to hear.
Some are already packed up well,
Others are at it, most pell mell.

Though there is still more work left to do,
Before we turn away no longer face to face,
Its time to climb aboard the bus and the plane.
We go back home to give witness in our daily place.

We will not soon forget what we've done,
As we've come to this fair land.
We've more reason to put love in action
And for Jesus always to take our stand.

February 11, 2006

Love in Practice

So dear Lord, do this real,
Thy gift of love in us seal,
Let us grow in grace every day,
Put love in practice on our way.

We can but live each long day,
But each moment we fairly pray,
"Lord, let us rejoice ever in Thee,
Not be led of evil, but by Thee".
Father, Son and Holy Spirit,
Three in One, thy will do it.

This day we live and not tomorrow,
One day at a time lends every sorrow,
But each day lends its every hour,
Fair it can be, like a flower.

Lo 'tis He who sets the pace,
Let's run with Him our daily race,
Lord, help us to live one day at a time,
Walk by thy side with faith sublime.

Love Sent

Oh God and Father, what have you done,
In the giving of your only Son?
Sending love that gives itself on the cross,
And battles with death till the Victory is won!

In it all you dare to promise us,
That as You whisper to us our name,
You show us a love coming from above
That helps us never to be the same.

We find ourselves as we follow Him,
And seek to walk in the ways He walks.
We find our strength coming from God
As we talk to Him like He talks.

December 1997

Making It Happen Today

Annual conference time is coming near;
That means preparing minds to be clear.
There is much to weigh and clarify;
Where to put our emphasis, and also why.

What do we expect to do next year?
Will we make it really clear?
So all of us can have a part,
Making it happen with all our heart.

More folk brought to know the Lord.
Helping the new believers also share the Word.
It can do much to renew the church,
Give it steady stamina instead of one big lurch.

A lurch of faith may help to start,
But it takes more to feed the heart.
It takes rest, steady growth, and study too,
To help faith grow and feed the ever new.

So let's get at it and keep telling the story,
How God reaches down from His glory;
To remind us that He is always here anew,
It depends on us to use our eyes and hearts too.

So lead on, Oh Great Jehovah and Holy Father,
Giver of our Redeemer, Your Son, our Brother.
He stills teaches us through His Living Word;
We read it, believe it, share it – the greatest story ever heard.

November 20, 2007

Mary My Darling, Come On Darling

Workin' – we've done it, and waitin' lots more;
Pinin' – we've known it, and livin's been a chore;
All because we're apart, and can't share anymore.

Chorus:
Come on darling, let's go to the mountains;
Come on baby, let's visit the sea;
Come on honey, let's run in the meadow;
I'm thinking of you and you're thinking of me.

Why do you miss me, why I you, my dear?
It's because you're up there and I'm way down here.
It's because there no cuddlin' and there's so little cheer.

Now, when you get here and I see you every day,
I'll love you as always and in many a new way.
If you answer right a question, you'll be here to stay.

Now, now that you're here, life's most full of glee;
I can't love you enough, nor can you me, you see.
The honeymoon is forever and we're as happy as can be.

1990s

Mary, Mary, Mary

Mary, Mary, what did you say
When you put Jesus on the bed of hay?
Mary, Mary, what did you sing?
Did the bells of heaven for you ring?
Mary, Mary, what did you see
When you dreamed of what He would be?
Mary, Mary, what did you find
When you searched your heart and mind?
Mary, Mary, what did you whisper
When little Jesus was only a lisper?
Mary, Mary, what did you promise
When you stood with doubting Thomas?
Mary, Mary, what did you think
When you heard them say, "He has risen?"
Mary, Mary, what did you shout
When from that tomb He walked out?
Mary, Mary, come walk with us
There is victory amid all the fuss.
It is true! He is alive! He is risen!
'Tis God's answer! 'Tis Holy leaven!
'Tis the Spirit, one of the Three!
There's more wonder to come for you and me.

May 6, 2008
(Hank, Geryl and Angie are here)

Mirador

We are waiting in the church,
For the coming of the hearse;
This is a rainy afternoon,
We hope it doesn't get any worse.

We've come, afraid we would be late,
Wondering why they said at eight,
Then it was true love and now word,
It's now three, it's going to be late!

So what do you do while you wait?
Why you play that guitar and sing;
Maybe by singing God's praises,
Will help them come and bring.

Here we are a car full waiting,
In all we reached to number seven.
We are not here to cry and sigh,
We are celebrating an entry into heaven.

Our good friend and Pastor Manuel,
Has ended His battle on earth,
Now it is new life with God,
For this is the result of the second birth.

November 6, 2007

More Than Conquerors

May this love I have for You, My God,
Never stop growing in any part;
May it make all the difference every day,
Spreading joyous love from an overflowing heart.

All things take on new meaning;
Underneath the sure foundation there is no fear,
We are more sure of who we are
And we know more why we are here.

We now find in living a new quality,
We are sure eternity begins here and now;
We do not have all the answers,
But we have a faith that knows the how.

The difference we find in our Savior,
He is our Lord of Life, and King.
Rich relationship we have with Him;
Does to our life new victories bring.

Paul said we are more than conqueror
Through the new faith we know.
The doubts we may once have had
Can in our hearts no longer grow.

We are in Him and He is in us,
Together we make a winning team.
More satisfaction comes each day
Than before we could ever dream.

November 17, 2007

Mother's Day At The Center

A dancing leaf here, a dancing leaf there,
Then they dance by three and four;
The dance becomes a real deluge
As the clouds open wide their doors.

It was a silent time this afternoon,
All was at peace and blessed rest.
At once, there came the abundant storm
Flooding the birds in many a nest.

After the storm passed, rumbling on,
Mother birds hopped right off to shake.
The water flew to every side
And did many a sleepy one wake.

Back on the nest in place again,
Mother bird settles in for the night.
She's a picture of real patience.
Next morning things will be most bright.

Costa Rica Mother's Day
August 15, 2003

Mr. Wren

Look there, a little bird, a wren, just flew in through the hallway door and here into the living room! He is stepping and dancing around there by the vase and the television.

There is a bird house, a ceramic one, on top of the TV, but he hasn't found it. I make loud noises, thinking to shoo him out, but he just goes on back behind the TV to see if the cartoon factory is back there. He just keeps on examining back there.

Finally he comes out and flies down to the floor by the outside door. He thinks he can go under the door! But he won't fit, and besides a little brown iguana with an orange stripe down his back has come to investigate.

Mr. Wren flits and dances about, putting on a show before he flies up and lands on the top of the half-screen door. He sizes up the world and decides to go out there into that great big green sea of life to discover what he has missed while he ventured inside a house, entering and leaving by the front door.

Who cares if he didn't knock or ask permission!

My Ever Present Savior and Friend

Jesus, My every present Savior and Friend,
The one who knows me best,
After that full day of work,
I lay me down to rest.

You are ever a comfort to my heart,
You are ever and forever in my soul.
Life does have its many trials,
But You forgive and make us whole.

Though we may become very broken,
Unable to be at our best for Him;
His healing touch makes us whole,
To cast aside that debilitating whim.

We are made more than conquerors
In all the tests life does us give.
His strength and power abides in us
As day by day we gladly live.

March 9, 2007

My Friend

I lay me down to sleep.
It has been a trying day.
So many different tasks to do,
With Jesus on the way.

Had it not been for Him
Walking by my very side
To help me to make right choices,
I would have walked the highway wide.

He is with me in the morning,
He dines with me at Monday bright.
He continues with me in the afternoon
And grants me rest at night.

My wonderful friend is Jesus,
The blessed Savior of us all.
No more than a thought away,
To guide us lest we fall.

Let us praise Him now and forever,
Never getting tired to exalt His name.
His Good News ever on our lips,
We declare his glorious fame.

Not only is this for me;
It is for each and every one of you.
He makes life richer by the moment
While our hope is ever new.

This hope turns into assurance,
Our faith is stronger than our sight;
There reigns within our immortal soul
The desire to ever do it right.

March 9, 2007

My Lord, What a Flower

My good Lord, what a precious flower!
This lily comes all decked out in threes.
Six stems arch out into a bulging bloom;
Each bloom has six petals, if you please.

From the middle of each bloom extend six white flowers;
At the end of these fingers is an arc, all pollen laden.
Then there is one longer spike from the very center,
Thus making stems, fingers and spike number seven.

The big green stem thus produces six bloom-bearing spikes,
Which reach up and out, arching with complete grace.
Oh, the harmony of it all, threes, sixes and one seven.
Six pure white blooms with six curvy petals, each in its place.

How perfectly God makes each of His flowers,
And tenderly forms, with love, each little face.
What glorious beauty He shares with us all,
As He creates life with joy, on His planet Earth, as well as
outer space.

Next morning, Friday, not all the blooms have stood the night,
Blown by the fan, the air has weathered and taken its toll.
Today there will be but three for us to enjoy.
Time catches us all, but in Him we rest while the seasons roll.

Even now, our dear Mother Russell lies bedfast.
Her body there, worn and weathered, racked with pain,
Struggles on, as now and then she becomes alert;
Touched by God, she is refreshed like thirsty soil enjoying
summer rain.

And what do we see as we look around us?
Do we find holy numbers-threes, sixes, and a seven?
Do we sense that through flowers He speaks to us?
And do we feel His gentle power preparing us for Heaven?

June 8, 1997

Our Mother Russell was called Home by God on June 10, 1997

My New Shirt

I have a 3XXX T-shirt;
It came as a gift to me.
It reads "Keep working for the Lord"
That's the best way to become free.

Oh, I know the greater truth,
We are workmen together with God;
We are partners with Him in mission
From Sacramento to Cape Cod.

This T-shirt also reads along
"The pay isn't very much
But the retirement plan, oh man,
Is really out of this world" for such.

This biggie I'll wear while I sleep
And may also, while I work.
That way the world can see
That Christians do not shirk.

2008

My New Used Shirt

I do not know who has worn this shirt,
Nor from whence it came to me.
But one thing sure, it fits just right,
I'm as happy as a man could be.

You see my other long-sleeved shirts
Kept me warm when it was cold.
They've just grown tattered, thin, and faded,
Even worse, if the other half were told.

So it's time to blow the whistle loudly,
A substitute has come to play the game.
Its black and white lines form a checkered figure;
Now, would you help me give it a name?

It's soft-like as medium flannel shirts come,
Smooth, warm, and friendly to the touch.
We're going to form a real good friendship
And enjoy being together ever so much.

Why take all this time to write about a shirt?
"Couldn't you spend it better writing about something other?"
Well, I don't rightly think it's a loss of time;
You see, a shirt really "sticketh closer than a brother."

May 18, 1997

My Twelve Red Roses

I sit here alone with my red roses;
The twelve have now become seven.
'Tis true their beauty shall long be remembered;
Into my life, they have brought new leaven.

Yesterday and today they've dropped and bent;
They've had to give up the ghost.
But I've rescued the soft tender petals,
They're precious to me, the whole host.

My wife, my own, my dear loving friend,
Thank you again for all of your caring.
You've been so wonderfully good to me;
Thank you for all of your sharing.

Now listen, you men, and you ladies, too.
Let's cherish those scents that tickle our noses.
Let's give the gifts our partners will cherish;
But above all, sometimes let's give them twelve roses.

November 20, 1997

Never Alone

All alone in the office,
Yet never alone,
Thou art ever with us,
Your honor no limited zone.

In a whisper you're heard,
In an instant you're there,
But it's also most true
You're always everywhere.

Be God! Just Be!

* * * * * * * * * *

Some dream of being alone,
Some wish they weren't,
Some dream of starting a fire,
Some are already most burnt.

Those who live with Jesus,
By day and also by night,
Never even have to worry,
The battle is His for right.

"Ain't you glad you're in it to win it with Him?"

* * * * * * * * * *

I will no more be lonely,
I'll be happy all the while.
The answer is most easy,
The Texans gave me their smile.

One thing about enormous Texans,
There's always lots more space;
But greater still is something else,
It's that Texan's sense of grace.

August 31, 2003

New Appointments

The bishop stood up to speak.
Said he, "This is how we're going to work."
He read the appointments of the District Superintendents,
And caused them all to go berserk.

They all reacted and some over-reacted.
They revealed their great surprise.
Some also fainted or had an attack;
What a change showed in their eyes.

After reading a number of the appointments,
Pandemonium almost broke out.
We saw that the Bishop was joking.
We laughed, ooh'd and aah'd even with a shout.

Well that is one way to get the attention
When it comes to Methodist preachers.
It breaks up the sheer monotony
And reaches even to the bleachers.

Centro Metodista Alajuela – General Conference
December 2, 2005

No Other Savior

I know no other Savior
Who would die to set me free.
There's no other love so great,
To give me real liberty.

He alone took up the cross
To take away my sin.
Then gave me the power
Against temptation to win.

Great glory to my Jesus,
I love Him with my all.
He's the one who died for me;
And stoops my name to call.

The way He speaks my name,
I know He is my friend.
I must tell others all about Him,
And a helping hand to others lend.

2003

No Wonder They Call Him Savior

No wonder they called Him the Savior;
No wonder they called Him Lord;
He gave them a face for the Father;
In Him, God spoke His best word.

For God spoke through Him right plainly
Of mercy and forgiveness He spoke.
Of tender love He shared like a shepherd;
On the cross where His heart broke.

The answer to sin and sad separation
From the Creator, Father of the world;
The lost, the least and the helpless,
Share in His Kingdom with banners unfurled.

He's the One who touches our bodies
When we're all racked with pain.
The Healer who is eternally present;
No need to go by car or by plane.

A cup of cold water to the tired and thirsty;
A show of kindness and love in His name;
All this while done for the needy,
Becomes as done to Him, the same.

No limit is there to His servant,
In what can be shared, spoken and done.
Through service to others our ministry,
We witness to the great victory He's won.

The Spirit comes daily to convince us,
Just like Jesus promised and said,

He's our companion all along life's journey;
He's God's answer: He's risen from the dead.

We worship no poor, defeated Savior.
We claim no weak helpless Lord.
We've privilege to share in His victory;
Marching to His music, by note and by word.

There's no redemption, no salvation through another;
Through Him we see God's face.
He's the answer to our needs as sinners;
To us and to the whole human race.

No wonder we call Him our Savior,
No wonder we call Him our Lord!
He is for us the way to the Father;
His name's the sweetest we've ever heard.

July 12, 1988

Nonsense

Tomorrow is another day,
And I'm already behind;
I've been looking for myself,
And me I cannot find.

I need to tell myself,
If me I am able to find,
That I am to stop hiding,
Or I am going to lose my mind.

There is a chance for me,
To prove to some of my friends,
That they are wrong when they say,
He's really full of loose ends.

I know it's they who are wrong,
For I caught them singing in a mirror,
But what I could see of them,
Was hidden by my face I fear.

February 2007

Of What Spirit

I do not know of what spirit you see;
I spoke out of frustration and not from love.
More care must be given before I speak,
So I can really say what it is I seek.

I'm finding it difficult to remember names and faces,
There are getting to be far too many of these cases.
Maybe there are answers for ancients like me,
I don't want to get worse than I be.

I hope it's associated with being tired,
Because if it isn't then I'll get fired;
For I intend to get some good rest,
And then try to be at my best.

Life in the eighties has much in its favor,
You've had time to live and taste its flavor;
Then too you have a real sense of gratitude –
Our thanks to God is seen by our attitude.

We can take time to think and to read,
'This keeps us from admittedly goin' to seed;
Then above all thanks to God for being here,
For being up to date with a conscience clear.

September 2007

On A New Morning

The face of a flower is lovely to behold.
It's even more meaningful than what mother told.
The skies so azure blue are ever a real blast,
But they are greater still with half-filled clouds in contrast.

The waking birds rejoice as they begin to sing,
Their music fills the morning air, melody on the wing.
The sleepy farmer hears it all, and also a lowing cow,
He hurriedly puts on his britches, the calf is hungry now.

So many things to do, and that all at once.
His wife's counseling is true, he is but a dunce,
Refusing to set an orderly way to do all his chores,
He finds himself all mixed up, going in and out the doors.

Poor man, he hasn't time to look at all the glory,
But when he becomes organized it will be quite another story.
Then the wife who criticized him for being but a dunce,
Will find herself getting breakfast on time, doing everything at once.

May 8, 2008

On Knowing Jesus

I would that you know Him, too;
That you would follow Him every day.
He is the greatest of all companions;
Let His love permeate your heart and stay.

His welcome is a forever call,
Once you get to know Him well.
You will desire with more passion, too,
Once you love Him more than tongue can tell.

November 16, 2007

On The Field

The most important thing on the mission field
Is not the salary we earn or are paid;
It's found in the faith of hearts and smiling faces,
In the new life being lived, with the foundation laid.

For there shall rise and grow His living church,
On the field it shall prosper beyond belief.
If people are helped to find faith in God,
Faith in Jesus Christ our Savior, conqueror of sin and grief.

Not only is it important to sing and sing,
What we sing must also be found in what is wrought.
The life we live speaks louder than our words.
We reveal that there is a power which Jesus brought.

On that cross for everyone He suffered and died.
"How much does God love you?" "This much," He said,
Spreading His arms, they nailed His hands and feet.
Into God's hands He gave Himself and they pronounced Him dead.

They laid Him in a new tomb wrapped in linen.
Doing what they could, but feeling it was in vain.
They had already forgotten in their helpless grief,
That he had said, "And I shall rise again."

This is the message the whole world needs –
That life is worth living on this earth;
Lifted in the power and beauty of eternal love;
Love that is born in us – a second birth.

Life begins here that never ends;
Eternity begins for us right here and now.
It is a beginning walk toward perfection;
We begin it and stay in it with Him, that's how.

2005

On the Run

It's early morning and I'm on the run,
No time for a decent meal,
I'll grab the last of that jello salad,
And run to get under the wheel.

Pineapple and fresh peaches,
Join with the grapes and cherry,
Mixed with the jello powder,
Made and chilled, it's time to make merry.

Oops, I forgot to count the pills
Which I have to take;
No time to take them now,
Maybe – unless there's a coffee cake.

2007

One More

One more high mountain to climb,
One more swift river to cross,
One more long mile to trot,
And that without a good "hoss!"

This is no place for babies;
No room here for the faint.
This requires real dedication;
You can't claim to be what you "ain't."

People are waiting to find Jesus;
They may see Him living in you.
Take up your cross and follow;
Let your faith ever be strong and true.

Here there can be no make-believe,
You are His ambassadors this day.
Keep close to Him as His servant,
Reach out to others after you pray.

Joy will spring up in your living;
Strength will come to your heart.
You're called into His service;
He'll never from you depart.

Praise God forever, dear brother;
In your will let His Kingdom reign.
We're in it to win it with Jesus,
And the battle is His to gain.

Only He

There is no end, it is always,
Here we whet ourselves on the go.
We are following, following Him – Jesus;
He died for me, I love Him so.

Now I can do no less than follow;
He has promised to help me grow.
He points our faces to where the sun rises,
He calls us, "Follow me and grow."

Like the tree planted by the water,
Like the good seed sprouted and growing.
We are in the battle with Him,
We are out there always good and sowing.

Only yesterday He helped me see
I was stubborn, wanting to be first.
Now I desire to take my turn,
I'm so full of love, I'm ready to burst.

It's amazing the change He makes;
I want to do what is right, right now.
He stirs my best self into flame,
As I go into service before Him and bow.

There is only, only, only He.
There is none other like my Lord.
Even in the darkest hour ever,
There He is accepting me in accord.

March 27, 2007

Only One

There is only one God,
There is only one King,
There is only one Savior,
Who does our salvation bring?

There is only one Spirit,
Sent from the Father above,
He is with us all daily,
Sharing the Trinity's love.

October 17, 2007

Oranges

When I was a little child,
I thought it would almost heaven be,
If I could have a Sunkist orange,
Or better still, have in my yard, a tree.

And now, more than seventy years later,
It is my precious special lot
To have tangerines, lemons, and grapefruit too,
Plus juice and navel oranges on my plot.

Some would say, "Well, how can that be?"
And others would shout, "Good luck!"
But I'm most grateful to my Heavenly Father,
Who lets me, citrus from our trees, pluck.

I just gladly give thanks daily you all,
That what I longed for as a humble child,
We as a family then could not buy them
Now I do have that high privilege. It's wild!

July 23, 2004

Our Best Always

No need to worry about tomorrow,
Today makes enough demands.
It's enough to give it our best;
He's right here with us -- good lands!

His presence makes all the difference.
He's with us, come day or night.
His power can be felt, just listen;
Inside He's turning on His precious light.

A gleam starts shining in our eyes,
A glow is growing in the heart,
Our eagerness to be out on the road,
Hurries our pace much faster than the start.

There is always enough to fill our time,
So choose excellence every day.
Quality we would choose in our thoughts,
Love we would include all the way.

The mountains are His
And the trees also.
Blue skies speak His name;
His vastness in love is never just so-so.

May 8, 2008

Our Eternal Creator

God is right here at hand,
He needs no introduction at all.
He is always present every moment,
He never needs to place a call.

He may touch our opened heart.
He may come at once to mind.
All doors are opened, none closed to Him,
He's at home with every kind.

Because He has called us to be born
He is interested in what we be.
We each are special to Him, our Creator,
He does really love us, both you and me.

While this fact may surprise us,
Still with all our hearts we do believe;
For the Eternal Creator, who is also Father,
Is He who sends the vast love we receive.

He may choose to send it indirectly;
We may discover it through others;
There we see Him always working
In the lives of our sisters and brothers.

November 2007

Our Gentle Master's Timing

How often we plan to do as we like,
In the way we think is the best;
Then the Gentle Master of all of life
Puts all that we've planned to the test.

And as we get to work, listen and pray,
So many things come to the light.
We find our timing may be quite wrong,
Then God whispers the answer, and it's right!

So many things begin to fall into place,
While order becomes our gift from the King;
New possibilities appear in the united task,
As we all share the visions we bring.

We become one in Him as we work along;
The task makes sense to one and all.
He bonds us together and no one shirks;
We are united without one dividing wall.

"Ye are mine and I've chosen you.
Let me guide you in all that you do."
You'll find it best if we work together;
We'll be a team in all kinds of weather.

No talents are best, we need them all.
Without anyone's effort, down comes the wall.
We're supporting each other the best we can,
Through His love in us, for our fellow man.

December 1997

Our Way – Your Way

Think what the world would be like,
If all of us really had our way.
It would be an unrecognizable, egotistical sight,
With everyone pulling and hauling and having their say.

It's great that God early, let mankind see,
That left alone, a tower of Babel is the fruit.
Man is made in His image, that's very true,
But each one needs help, his instrument to toot.

Our Father gave us such a wonderful gift,
When He sent us His Son, among us to live.
His words and ways of kindness and of love,
Help us really see it is more blessed to give.

Once we've been forgiven and are really turned around,
His daily Presence becomes our guiding light;
And you wouldn't begin to recognize us all,
His harmony in and among us creates such a wonderful sight.

Jesus, our Lord, we know we only see a part;
Your plan is so very much larger than we know.
But the Kingdom of God, your Kingdom of love, we cherish;
We want love's powerful changes in us more and more to show.

Take each of us and in us create even more,
That spirit of love that helps each of us our instrument to play;
That we really become your symphony in action,
Where the music of your church, your body, fills both night and day.

July 27, 1996

Overcomers

Awakened in the night hours,
There is little peace of mind;
Old man flu has a hold of me,
Peace is most hard to find.

The coughing and the straining,
Make the voice-box wonder when
It's going to be quiet once more,
And we are able to rest again.

Of course, having this part of life's battle,
Is part of the price to be here to stay,
Life is often kept going by struggle,
Whetted on obstacles all along the way.

We would not only know comfort,
Difficulties are blessings in disguise;
In the struggles we are kept growing,
Made ready for each surprise.

"You are more than conquerors," wrote Saint Paul,
"Through Christ who strengthens you so;"
A marvelous companion is our Living Lord;
Great this is to experience, and to know.

Patience, Patience

Patience, patience, wait, wait,
One of the hardest things to do.
But to have patience under pressure,
Is a challenge to me and to you.

It will help if we trust in God,
And use well the times we wait;
It may well be that He's in waiting,
To open to us a better gate.

We have so very much to learn,
But if we give Him half a chance,
He will give us His ways on a loan,
To help us our life of service to enhance.

Then when He does, we must know
We are to be ready to bend.
Flexible and malleable by His grace;
His love and His wisdom He too, will lend.

Planning

It is one thing to say it,
It is quite another to be it,
But if you don't depend on Him,
You will never have the help to do it.

The greatest is that we can't do it all,
It was never meant for us to do it alone,
Only with Him can we ever do it at all,
Trying to do it alone, we only stumble and fall.

He is the One, the only One,
Who can ever help it come to be;
Only He, the great physician, can help us to see,
He is the only One who has set us all free,
From our shackles of sin we are made to flee.

He touches us to send us marching,
Discontent to take it easy any more.
He leads us to the fields of Holy Harvest,
Where we shall be at work forevermore.

His call is most tender, even as a whisper,
Though it could be a blast for all to hear.
He prefers sometimes to treat us tender,
As He spreads abroad in our hearts, good cheer.

Dear God, you treat us tender,
Though we are slow to hear,
You keep sending to us ever,
Your Great News of good cheer.

Salvation is a real blessing,
Meant for all of us to partake;
He gave Him life that we might really
Believe in Him, and work for His name's sake.

August 2007

Poem to Paula

Now, I look there in that waste basket;
What is it there I see?
Four heart stamps made of lovely roses,
All smiles and looking up at me!

They're on a bright blue envelope,
I must rescue them for sure.
Why, the letter is from Paula,
A card for Dad, with love so pure.

I'll take these four heart stamps;
Cut them out with her address;
Use them as my Bible book mark;
How often they will me bless.

Thank you, Paula, for your love,
And for all your patience, too.
I'm writing you a long delayed letter;
Oh, how much I do love you!

September 12, 2000

Project Venecia

Where will this project lead us;
This effort of Tico-Yankee cooperation?
Will we reach out into the villages
From which the youth come for education?

This must all be but the beginning
Of what God intends there to be.
In this section of Northern Costa Rica,
We're on the move, you wait and see.

There's a new drive and a new spirit;
One that unites us into action with joy.
It's great to provide for the new generation,
Handles that they can take and employ.

So here we are hard at it daily,
All this week we will be doing our best.
We may become tired, bruised, and exhausted,
But next month we will be able to rest.

Just think that in a week's time
We have come this far down the road.
It hasn't hurt any of us from the straining,
We have all carried our part of the load.

Some of us are old and quite limited;
But we can plan, encourage, and give.
Others are better able to do the hard work,
We all will rejoice together as we live.

Yes, we have come together these few days,
We've united our efforts, our enthusiasm too;
It has been a most worthwhile adventure;
I'm so glad God led us together, aren't you?

June 30, 2007

Questions – Have you Found Your Star in the Sky?

Have you found your star in the sky?

Have you found the Holy child?

Have you given Him your life?

While your heart beats high and wild?

Rain Rest Read

The music of the falling rain
Plays on the tired senses.
It soothes the aching muscles,
And slumber quickly dispenses.

One who gives it full permission
To capture his sincere decision;
He's found with head on the desk,
While others laugh in derision.

But deep rest it also brings,
New joy from being relaxed.
Who cares what the cost may be,
It's worth being fully taxed.

Rest is the spring of new life,
A siesta daily is good tonic;
If it were anything better,
One would travel supersonic.

So take it easy my dear friend.
Take time to get real rest.
It regenerates your whole system,
Makes you feel at your best.

Then, too, while you ponder,
Do rest in the risen Lord;
Let Him speak straight to you,
While you read his Holy Word.

July 6, 2004
Tired and listening

Red, Red Roses

With six red roses and a smile of love,
He came hiding them behind his back.
He said, "They're especially for you, my dove,"
And right then and there, I thought I'd crack.

No man had ever given me flowers,
Much less an armload of red, red roses.
This is long after our marriage and showers –
"Just think, it's a honeymoon for always!" he proposes.

"Can this be for me, oh my dear, dear Lord?
Red roses on just another common day?"
And he greets me with such a loving word.
It leaves me speechless; I've nothing I can say.

Then all at once I begin to sob and cry;
Well, at least deep down inside of me I do.
I look at him with love, letting out a sigh,
And whisper "I'm so glad, my beloved, that you're you."

Written in 1993 for Mary Maria

Reducing

Where has all the blubber gone?
I'm actually a little trimmer.
Some more of this practice,
And I will even be slimmer!

It doesn't take so much doing;
You just start eating less,
And when you are offered seconds
You forget how to say "Yes."

Then those fatty foods are left alone,
The white breads and sweets are a "No."
Go heavy on the fruits and vegetables –
Pronto! Then it all begins to show.

The rolls seem to roll on off;
The shape is better seen again.
You recognize the man in the mirror
And you can greet him with a grin.

May 8, 2008

Relationship

Oh boundless, precious love divine!
What security, joy and comfort you give.
How do those who do not of that partake,
Ever find that without which we cannot live?

We are made for a vital relationship with Him;
No other help ever does us satisfy.
Real peace and joy we find not anywhere,
Until we, His love and fellowship try.

God has made us for Himself;
He knows best what we need.
Did He not start our lifeline yonder?
Are we not also from old Adam's seed?

Yes, our eternal relationship in His hands;
Has us restless until we rest in His care.
He is our Owner, Savior, Lord and Friend;
Once with Him, we seek no other lair.

November 13, 2005

Remember Jesus Christ

Remember Jesus Christ who was raised from the dead.
That colors everything!

Remember Him!
You think of everything differently because of
His touch, His concern, His determination, His obedience,
His will to do the will of His Father, His love for all people.
Beggars, lame, sick, crippled blind, poor, rich, sinners,
All are people. For children especially, too. Riches are not
enough. This is the message we take.

Be ready – Get ready!
Don't miss the bus!
Don't try to knock on the door of Heaven as a stranger.
How badly you will feel!

How great is His love
Forever and ever.

May 8, 2008

Right Here Beside Me

At two and fifteen and more,
A visitor came to this your chair.
He looked for his lovely mate,
But she just wasn't there.

So he decided to up and leave,
To seek her elsewhere.
Maybe she has gone to sleep –
And that not in a chair.

So away, I gave in a bit
After writing on this little pad.
I've come to tell you "I love you,"
I'm trying not to be sad.

I will go and look elsewhere.
Goodness, could it really be
That you were there as I arose,
Right there sleeping beside me?

I'm a gone man by the kitchen route;
The other door is locked. Night, night!

February 2007

Roses are a Blessing

Roses are a blessing from God,
Each with its own special perfume.
Every color and tint blessing our sight
So far beyond what we assume.

A bouquet of roses graces a busy desk,
Beckoning all to take a smell.
What heavenly aroma it shares with us,
Whispering how God does all things well.

Thank you, Father, for your love,
Your tender presence, forever sharing.
Thy Rose of Sharon Thou didst send;
Blessed salvation comes through your caring.

Touched by the beauty from Thy hand,
May we reflect Thy bounteous grace.
Like roses, let us open wide,
Revealing eternity's rapture on each face.

Salt Water

Salt water is drawing out
The meanness from my thumb;
The color of that little fellow,
Is like a reddish, purple plum.

Maybe I should be using
A piece of pig fat instead;
When it comes to common things like this,
You've really gotta use your head.

The other modern medicines that I have used
Under the visitin' nurse's care,
Haven't seemed to help all that much,
So I'm going to use another pair.

Soap and water helps prepare the way,
Salt in hot water has a special drawing power,
It helps if one will only sit,
Keeping that thumb submersed for an hour.

Well, maybe not all that long –
But really soaking it a good long while.
Discovering salt water as a friend,
Helps to heal in a humble style.

Maybe that is part of what Jesus meant,
When He said with a lot of clout,
"O ye are the salt of the earth,"
So go help draw the meanness out.

Of course, we know how much God wants
To count on us, to give flavor to all of life.
That, we hope to do, through showing love,
And making it really rife.

Sharing With Others

Sometimes, men, I'm afraid to talk,
Lest I be ashamed of what I say.
But the Spirit nudges me onward,
To share with others on the way.

For if we do not show and tell,
Limited will be the witness;
We're called to let Him live in us,
May God's Kingdom be our business.

So, let us speak beyond the rambling,
Let us feel free in word and deed,
Let His message reach through our living,
When with others who are in need.

And when others lend a helping hand,
When they ask what they can do,
Be with us in all our teaching,
To share your example clear and true.

Sit Back, Listen, Receive

Sit back, lean back, open that will;
Let Him come, be you yielded and still.
Let there be no talk, not a word,
Listen for His coming, His whisper heard.

He needs no words, you feel Him here;
He stirs your soul as He brings good cheer.
You sense His grace close every hour,
You receive His care and redemptive power.

October 31, 2005

Sleep and Rest

What do you do at a time like this,
When your strength seems gone away?
Well, probably before you go to rest,
You should take some time to pray.

That way you can give yourself time
To recuperate and restore a bit,
So that when you do go to retire,
You can really give yourself to it.

Pressure and stress are rascals,
They tie us in difficult knots.
There is always more to be done now,
Pleading for attention, are too many "oughts."

Sleeping can also be a game;
You train how to get all relaxed.
You are ready to begin to play,
Your mind is, at least, untaxed.

It does help to get beneath the covers
With a real desire to rest;
That way you are really relaxed,
And later, you can just be at your best.

July 19th

Sleep On, Mary

I sit here and watch you sleep,
The morning light invades our room.
It's time to rise up and meet the day,
So let us both go, our faces to groom.

You turn over once to cover your head;
You sink further in sleep, even to snore;
But it can't be long that you can compete
With that neighboring machinery's roar.

So you give up the struggle with a sigh,
Reach for The Book and start to read.
Nighttime is over, a new day to face,
The Word of God helps you meet your need.

I love you, yes love you, yes.

David and Linda's House
Autumn 1997

Soaked

I wonder how many are the raindrops
That have fallen on this farm today.
They've been every size, and ever so many;
I believe the storm is deciding to stay!

For sure the Maker of each little raindrop
Has been most generous, and all is wet.
Soaked is quite the better word to use,
From dawn to noontime, and now to sunset.

Should we go to sleep with the soft music,
The pitter patter, and the drumming on the roof.
At least maybe when we awake in the morning.
It will have finished and stay away, quite aloof.

If we awaken and it is still with us
It may become a real temporal.
Then we will be in for a soaking;
Things will become a real "boreal."

That means that it could be a "longie,"
One that will last for days, or even for weeks;
It will rain and pour and keep on raining.
It will get so that everything squeaks.

Then, of course, we will pray for sunshine,
Hoping for a change in the wet weather.
We'll do only what has to be done,
And wait awhile to do what we'd rather.

We'll not offer our hands in a greeting,
For that would mean that while we would squeeze
Everything would turn out real drippy,
Like the curdled milk in a sack hung for cheese.

All will sooner or later "come back to normal."
We will return to steady working again.
And after a while someone will be saying,
"Gosh, I wish it would hurry up and rain!"

December 1997

Some Glad Morning

Some glad morning we shall see
Jesus in the air,
Coming after you and me;
Joy is ours to share.

What rejoicing that will be
When the saints shall rise,
Headed for that jubilee,

Yonder in the skies.

Oh, what singing, oh, what shouting
On that happy morning
When we all shall rise.
Oh, what glory, Alleluia,
When we meet our blessed Savior,
In the skies.

Sometime When I Was Alone

So goes life when you're left alone,
You make do with what's around;
No standing on ceremony or style,
It's a simple life, with feet on the ground.

2007

Somewhere

Somewhere a voice is calling,
Someone is wanting to hear,
Somewhere that voice is pleading,
"I wish God would come more near."

Somewhere a heart is lonely,
Day is fast turning into night,
Somewhere faith is trying,
Still believing with all of its might.

Somewhere a soul is hoping,
That God will show His real face,
Thru Jesus, God still spreads His mercy,
On the far-flung human race.

Somewhere a life is loving,
Acts of kindness and grace everywhere,
Love is as normal as breathing,
Jesus has made that life care.

Somewhere a person is deciding,
To become a follower of the Way,
That person's heart is wide, wide open,
Jesus is Lord, by night and by day.

Yes, somewhere a voice is calling,
It's calling to you and to me,
The only Christ they hold in their hearts,
May be His picture, which in us, they see.

Son-In-Law, Son-In-Law

Late in the morning, early at night,
There is a phrasing often heard;
"Son-in-law, son-in-law, I love you."
To me that is precious, every word.

Sometimes it is with a humble cry,
Sometimes it is with a special whine.
"I can't help it," he often says,
You are my son-in-law, you're mine.

When you rub my back, you make me feel
As if I'm rich, though I haven't even a dime.
Sometimes you keep on massaging me;
I'm so glad you're my son-in-law, you're mine.

The man is rich who has more than one friend,
So you know who loves you all the time;
It is your old rich father-in-law,
I love you son-in-law, you're mine.

You heat my Postum when it is cold,
You even reheat my cooling soup,
You pamper me and also scold me,
But you ever help me cope.

Late in the evening, late at night,
What shout is more exciting than ice cream?
Ice cream? Ice cream? When? When? Where?
What joy is heard in that joyous scream.

So early in the morning every day,
At noon day, and even in the night;
I'm rich because I have a Christian father-in-law
Who loves God, and me, with all his might.

May 8, 2008

Soul Music

Listen, listen for a moment,
There seems nothing at all to hear,
Nothing is there a stir,
No reason a bit to fear.

It's time for soul music,
God's music is the best,
It's a whisper to the spirit,
It stirs the faithful chest.

It is sweet communion music,
At one with Jesus, our Lord,
All you have to do is listen,
There is nary a word.

He is here in the Spirit,
To heal, to comfort, to guide,
All we have to do is listen,
With the soul's door open wide.

He comes in to touch us,
We sense His real presence,
It is as Jesus promised,
The Spirit is God's essence.

We need to sit for hours,
We might even take a walk;
It is soul music with Him,
A new way for us to talk.

July 27, 2007

Spirit with Spirit

Coming back to my desk, I'm delighted,
The sun is playing with the leaves of the trees,
While the gentle breeze passes thru them,
They dance and make shadows here, if you please.

Those shadows play games on this sheet of paper,
Sometimes failing to show when the wind is strong,
Everywhere there is the feeling of gentle relaxation,
The cold weather is gone, and we all break out in song.

There is music that is only expressed in movement,
It may be that no sound at all is heard,
But the harmony bursts out in great enjoyment,
Like children lost in play without using a word.

This music might be termed soul music,
It is where Spirit with spirit met,
As Jesus said, "I have meat to eat that you know not of,"
So we have this union where Spirit with spirit met.

All this is related to the life of the Spirit,
Here we are but in the prelude with rapture;
Once freed later into life eternal of the Spirit,
There always will be so much more to capture.

November 26, 2007

Stop the Clock and Evaluate

Hey there, stop that clock from running,
Close up shop and rest a week.
It might be the best thing we ever did,
If we asked ourselves anew, "just what is it we seek?"

We've found that fame receives, and good fortune,
Escape most of us year after year,
What is there that's good to be said of us,
What have we accomplished – do we want to hear?

Are other people better because we're their friends?
Do they rejoice with the Lord in life?
Do they see the ways by which victories are won?
Do they have courage to show love amid the strife?

It's time to end this minute of writing,
My mind goes fuzzy, much need of sleep;
But it is not time to stop studying,
We pause and evaluate, oh, there will only be time to weep.

Then once we have evaluated well,
And faced up to reality with the Lord,
Let us open wide the doors of our lives
To Him, so He can speak to us His guiding word.

Others give time to God to write their agenda,
Others put their shoulders to work in His name.
Is it asking too much of us to learn from them;
Is it not His wise counsel urging us to do the same?
"Yup, thus saith the Lord!"

Storms

Dancing like leaves in a whirlwind,
Blown about by the swirling currents,
Surprisingly anxious to find their kind
Whipping about on tiptoe amid the torrents.

Storms, both make new friends, and leave others waiting,
Decisions are made instantly, and moment to moment.
It's time to forget about all the hating,
Persons become important regardless of race, color, or raiment.

Life and goods are to be protected and saved,
Sacrifices are made, really great spirits are born;
New ways for cooperation appear, new roads are paved,
And some things become discarded, their time 'most outworn.

Yet spontaneously the little leaves are called to dance
Lightly along with seeds that barely touch the ground.
It matters not the music, they still whirl and prance,
They seem to have been a whirlwind from springs unbound.

Be ready, ye who claim to live by the Spirit leading,
Have in you the incarnate Spirit of His Gentle Lord;
That when the storms come, you hear His pleading
And thus find yourself dancing by direction from above.

2005

Sunday

Sunday morning, time for church,
In this house a Holy search,
We would open eyes, mind and heart,
Be in the spirit from the start.

Though we've been with You all the week,
There is still great need, Your will to seek.
What should I do? Where to from here?
Please dear Lord, help make it clear.

Where I have failed, please forgive,
Help me closer to Thee daily live,
Make me mindful of all others;
Treat them as my sisters and brothers.

This is a special day to open Thy word,
Give attention to the greatest news ever heard,
Find in it the answers for life's test,
Treasures from it, keep in the breast.

Strengthened in spirit by word and song,
It's a special time all day long,
Time for fellowship, beyond saying "Hey,"
A chance to really listen to what others say.

Yet, sometimes it seems best to stay home;
Time to be alone and to nowhere roam;
Time to let God have His say
Without interruption, in His presence stay.

There is need for silence in our day,
Need to listen to what God has to say,
He may not speak both loud and long,
His message may come in a simple song.

But whatever it may be, whatever I say,
It will give us all marching orders for the day,
It will remind us to remember what He said,
I will never forsake you, I am with you instead.

September 5, 2004

Take This Day

Take the day given you by God,
Use it to His glory;
Listening to His word,
Saying you need not worry.

Sufficient unto this very day,
Is the evil thereof.
Look unto Him, His whisper,
Guiding you with love.

He's the Lord of the morning,
The keeper at night.
No evil can overcome you,
As you trust in his might.

Take This Life

Take this life and make it Thine,
Fill it with Thy spirit, Lord.
Let it praise Thee night and day
Revealing the power of Thy word.

Thou dost speak by tongues of men
Thy message to the whole wide world.
Possessing the beings of dedicated ones,
Thy glory Thou dost display, unfurled.

Flags of wonder shine in our face,
Banners of glory in the heart are bright.
Thy colors most marvelous in the soul
Speak through the countenance both day and night.

Peace Thou art to the troubled ones.
Those most burdened by work or fear
Respond to Thy word of peace and love,
As Thou dost whisper for them to hear.

Thou art He who hast created all;
Thou dost care for all that Thou dost make.
Thy Spirit comes in full display;
Here is my whole being for you to take.

2007

Take Time to Know Jesus

Take time to know and to love Jesus;
Spend it, too, with His Holy Word.
This is a very true invitation – admonition;
It's one of the greatest calls ever heard.

In our culture there are so many calls
To do this and that – to be successful.
But so many of these urgent invitations
End up leaving us with a life that's stressful.

You see, He's the author of all time;
To use it correctly is part of our biz.
We have to open the door to invite Him in;
If we're going to understand what it is.

This creation of His is made for fellowship;
We are given the privilege to know and love the Father.
If we miss out on this rich relationship,
Life ends up being to us a dreary bother.

But relationship with Him colors all else;
Everything takes on new meaning, new light.
This love and respect relation with the Father,
Helps everything else have meaning, and be right.

You see, God at Christmas gave us a baby,
With His great big heart of love opened wide.
Through Him, He has given to each of us;
One who not only walks before us, but is by our side.

December 20, 2005

Taking Five

Fully fatigued, not caring to move a muscle,
I stood there realizing that I could no longer hustle.
Too long and too far had I gone today,
Taking more than five to rest is the only way.

After all, the efficiency drops while being tired,
And being my own boss today, I say, "Rest, or you're fired."
Then later I would ask Papa to fire me up again,
Fresh as a daisy after resting, I could begin.

It's good if, when that built in whistle blows,
One will pay attention to the body that knows;
It has signs that speaks to the brain,
Telling that fellow to apply the brakes again.

Too often have I kept at it with my capers,
And have ended up with my nose in the papers;
Sometimes right there fast asleep at ten,
With my body saying "Stop now" or "Oh, when?"

Being obedient to that built in guide,
One can have faith to leave some things aside.
Then the next day a better work is done,
More days, then work becomes fun.

November 3, 2007

Taking Time

What a difference it does make,
Just three or four little hours.
It can even be less, of course,
With or without the flowers.

What am I thinking about?
Can it be listening to music or sports?
Would it be going for a visit,
Or playing a game on the courts?

No, it is not one of these,
Not at my age and on the run.
It is something far more simple,
It is more refreshing and more fun.

It is just putting on the pajamas,
Oh! Also connect the sleep machine;
Turning everything over to our Maker,
Let the old body play catch-up, that's keen!

July 27, 2007

Thank You God

Thank you, God, for all the help
You've placed upon this, your earth.
Help us take up the endless hunt,
To find aid for man's pain from birth.

We've only started on the road,
There's so much more to find.
Give us the strength to further the task,
With open heart and soul and mind.

Thank You, Mary

What must it have been for Mary,
Waiting there beneath that rugged cross,
Seeing her bleeding son eagle-spread?
Nothing less than all is loss.

Why this answer to His healing touch?
To His feeding the hungry all along?
To His teaching of the Kingdom of love?
Why this disgraceful display of wrong?

How dare they take my beloved son!
Why would priest and soldier join
To take the finest of all humanity;
To end His life in a display of wrong?

What system of rule and religion,
Both of Roman government and of Jew,
Dare with barefaced, evil cruelty?
Dear God, please give us justice new!

Such wrong is a bare-faced lie in action,
Putting the finest of Divine Love on a cross!
What hope for humanity could there be
When the powers of justice do such dross?

God in Heaven, Your God-sent Son
Hangs bleeding, high on those arms.
Was it for this that your angel
Told your plan to me with charms?

I can't believe it! There must be more!
This cannot be for us all, the end.
You must have more to say to us,
What more did your leaving send?

Did Mary believe and know by faith
That God had more yet to say
Through His beloved Son, His Messiah?
What will it be on the third day?

Her acceptance of the promises,
And in the words of Jesus revealed;
In her heart and tender spirit
She had believed that God was really real.
Thank You, Mary (cont'd)
She had heard the promises made.
She knew that He was God of power.
She held on with hope undefeated.
God had more to say in this hour.

With crushed hearts of hope and promise,
The Marys went to that holy garden.
There must be a message there waiting;
They dared not let their hopes harden.

So in faith they went that morn,
To the garden to do what they could.
Thank God they went there early
To find there what God would.

What God would do with Jesus!
Faithful in healing! Jehovah, His love!
Now there's life eternal beyond every grave!
He is the Risen One, freed from above.

Yes, my friend, you, like Mary, have reason to believe
In the God of stable, cross, and opened tomb.
Our Savior came to bring life eternal!
Come, believe, for all of us there is room.

April 2007

Thanks

I am thankful for you, dear friend,
And for all of your mercies with me.
May the King of all Thanksgivings
Be ever, oh ever so close, to Thee!

When this good day is all over,
And all the eating and fellowship is done,
Remember our love, like the leftovers,
Will linger to be enjoyed with great fun.

For neither distance, nor days passing by
Shall lessen the joy we both know,
Each hour shall continue to be precious,
While on purpose, we let our love show.

Thank you, dear one, for your friendship,
For letting me greet you by name
My heart's latchstring will ever be out and hanging,
And I'll always be glad 'twas you who came.

Should He call us while we are found parted,
Should we not be able to say adieu,
We will greet each other at the portals;
In Heaven we'll say, "Oh, I'm so glad to see you."

Thanksgiving 1997

The Apex

You are the apex of my creation.
How does this make you feel?
Are you as proud as a preened peacock;
Do you feel like you're best, like the big wheel?

On the other hand, does this humble you,
Since in you I've put my best efforts forth;
Planned you, sharpened you, perfected you,
Until you are able to prove your worth?

And do you see the rest of the world
As a part of your well-made home,
Do you love it and expect the best
As you pray, "Father, Thy Kingdom come?"

For I am still creating my universe,
And this is the way it will always be.
You had better get ready to love this place,
If you are going to come and work with me!

Creation continues throughout all time,
You are a Spirit given with a beating heart.
Use your senses, every last one, always
Be in our world and cherish it from the start.

Our universe is a tremendous garden;
Life is real and after death eternal life.
From stage to stage you experience it,
You are a spirit with possibilities ripe.

May 8, 2008

The Challenge To Remember To Believe and To Be

All this tendency in this our day
To do everything else, but celebrate His birth,
Stirs me to dedicate what time I've left,
To help welcome Him back to His earth.

Oh, He's here alright; it's we who are blind;
Our day fails to sense His Holy presence near.
His Holy Spirit is at work, oft unseen,
We walk with Him in love that casts out fear.

How crazy it is that God has to work
To keep trying to help men not try to be God.
How often we should look in the mirror
To see that we alone become nothing more than a clod.

How find ashes to ashes and dust to dust;
Ask yourself is that what you want really?
When you've lived your life self-determined,
Nothing else but dirt or hell or hopelessness, really.

The Chinese Are Coming

The Chinese are coming, yes siree,
Thousands of products from over the seas;
The price will be right, yes, really low,
It is all planned to make the sales grow.

The competition will be greater, fully worldwide,
People will see the products side by side.
It will be wise not only to look at the price,
But also to test the quality twice or thrice.

The competition will also make for better service,
This will come true in many a way;
The future is offering a new business world,
Where each of us will be found in this new day.

In our vision of a new world large enough
To adventure in it with folk from everywhere;
You and I must, as Christians, see His hand,
In the new day, holding His universe in His care.

We are called anew to be one world,
Our new communication expansion leads the way.
May we let God help us talk to each other,
As we walk together, learning to live in His love every day.

The Church at Los Chiles

Together we are beginning church construction in Los Chiles.
Alfredo and family open their home to me.
The Volunteers in Mission teams are working;
Each of us are busy as the proverbial bee.

It does touch one's heart at the real kindness,
The concern they all have for us and the church.
God's love is shed abroad in their hearts;
Without their special help we would be in a lurch.

The Spirit has taken over in our relations,
We are bonding together as a team.
More is being accomplished each new day,
As we hold His name and church in high esteem.

This beginning will turn into the norm;
The church structure is built, really made to serve.
Every new member shall in this place find
God calling him and her to use every muscle and nerve.

Here shall rise also His kingdom on this earth,
United in His love, made ready to live,
Telling abroad the Gospel of His grace,
Giving importance, not to what we have, but to what we give.

At Alfredo's, Los Chiles, Costa Rica

The Cross Makes the Difference

What can one say to praise the Lord,
For His grace shown on the cross?
No words of thanksgiving are enough,
For ridding our lives of all that dross.

Such wondrous love claims our all,
It bids our loyalty be ever new;
Such clear relief, such health wear,
Our life takes on a wondrous hue.

His companionship with us day by day,
Molds the strength of our beating heart.
We no longer walk life's way alone,
May His spirit never from us depart.

The cross of love born that day,
Made redemption for everyone most real.
We now worship Him, Lord of Love,
His presence with us we do ever feel.

Time will pass as we follow Him,
While His message to others we take.
We'll seek to share of that redemption power,
The difference His love in all does make.

November 24, 2006

The Jumpin' Methodists

Have to express the joy,
Have to praise my Lord,
Can't just do it by singing,
Gotta do more than use a word.

I've gotta jump with excess rhythm,
My heart's bursting – I've gotta shout!
My Lord has filled me up,
I've gotta jump, and kick sin out.

I wanna be satisfied in Jesus,
The gladness has gotta come out.
I'm just discovering for sure,
What finding Him is all about.

That's the reason I stomp and jump;
I've gotta be free, free from sin.
Out goes doubts and the devil,
Into my heart and life, Jesus comes in.

Some people think we've gone crazy,
They don't see how we're set free;
Free to express our great joy,
To let Jesus in us, others see.

It's release from tension and from doubt,
It's really quite a big jump.
We let the Lord Jesus know it
As new life comes in, and the old flies out.

August 2007

The Last Lily

The last lily was in the empty salt shaker vase,
Four petals on the hot pad,
One small arching leaf was left,
The last two petals looking sad.

The stem that held it all together,
Was getting most lonely I fear,
The water drop on the out reaching petal,
Would soon fall as a crying tear.

At least it graced the dining table,
And shared its beauty one more day.
The others of the special bouquet,
Had already gone by death's way.

How much we are like the flowers,
Given help to live a little longer;
But there comes the time to say goodbye,
Our weakened bodies can live no longer.

Lilies, like part of God's great beauty,
Such beauty He gives and returns to give;
Our beauty is released by our Savior,
As by faith, in Him we live.

2007

The Lord Touched Me in Bogue, Kansas

I met God in the half-lit morning
As I stopped my fast walking to pray.
The damp south wind was blowing;
    Would it bring us a rain today?

I didn't come to a real sudden stop,
    I sorta kept ambling along.
    I felt His presence with me
As he filled my heart with a song.

I stood on the road made of gravel
Amid the millions of grains of sand.
I realized that He had made them
And that He was holding me in His hand.

I looked up at the low flying clouds
Driven northward and most windblown.
I felt Him touching the winds within me,
As through the clouds, His sunlight shone.

He spoke to the harried-ness within me;
    To the desire to be at my best.
He told me to relax and to trust Him,
To fall into His strong arms and rest.

I kept walking on the road that was graveled;
    I gathered stones as I walked along.
Yes, the Lord reached out and touched me;
This morning He gave me a new song.

September 18, 1997

The Only Time Is Now

"I will do it tomorrow," we say,
And sometimes it's left undone.
We get too involved to keep the promise,
And we disappoint a growing son.

There are things that can't wait for tomorrow;
They must be done this very day.
The little hands left unattended
May later leave us with bills to pay.

The only time we have is now
To help loved ones, friends and more.
The differences empty promises make
Lead us to many a fast-closed door.

Do it now, if you will do some good,
Then leave the matter left untold.
If the Maker wishes for folk to know,
He will make it known threefold.

Do not blow your horn in public;
Never brag about what you've done.
Let the joy of doing and the thankful smile
Be enough to keep you on the run.

The only time you really have is now,
Tomorrow really never comes, I say.
Yesterday already has become history;
If ever you're to do His will, do it now, today!

Huntsville
October 29, 1999

The Stairway

I was seated on a stairway,
Writing stories about the Lord;
I heard a wee small voice,
Saying to me one little word.

The word was spoken in Spanish,
It was but a gentle appeal,
It came from a little fellow,
Asking for just a moment to steal.

He asked for me to help him down,
Yes, down all those seventeen steps;
They looked like a hundred to him,
And they didn't come in pairs.

I put down my pen and paper;
Standing up, I took his little hand,
We went down one step at a time,
Then he ran to beat-the-band.

I walked back up with a lighter step,
There was a tingle in my heart,
This child asked me, at eighty-one,
To help him get a fresh new start.

How ready are we to reach out,
To stop what we might be doing,
To help another one in need,
And thus let our Christian love keep showing?

Written at Methodist Center on steps down to basement
January 24, 2000

The Texans Came

The Texans came to our house;
They were a blessing to our eyes.
They worked, they healed, they prayed, they sang;
With them, each day brought a surprise.

The memories of their coming
Will last long and will linger.
When we hear of their return,
We'll count the days on each finger.

Once more each day will be too short
To hold all our laughter and our joy.
Work together becomes real fun
While our talents we all employ.

Ride 'em cowboy!

August 31 – September 2, 2003

The Vick's Vapor Rub Bottle

This morning at half past three,
I was trying to get relief, believe you me;
Short of breath, sweating it all out,
Sometimes wondering what it's all about.

After doing all the doctoring of myself,
Using what was both on and off that shelf,
As I was treating myself with Vicks vapor rub,
I was left with the lid of that little tub.

Just bought it, just about half in it than what used to be,
Twice as much cost for half as much – nothing for free.
Well, I dropped the bottom part and was left with the lid,
I wonder where it rolled over, and hid.

I just had to grin at that little plastic jar,
It couldn't have really rolled away all that far,
There it was sitting, with a wide open face,
It was waiting for me, a specimen of my race.

It sorta laughed at me for having come to look,
Expecting me to find it in some little nook.
Maybe I should learn from this a thing or two;
Where should I start to know what to do?

While you are thinking what to teach me,
Right now though, I'm going to see what I can see.
In that bedroom, I'm going to try to find my bed,
Then on that pillow, I'm going to rest this head.

Later… well, I found the bed and don't you know,
That pillow welcomed me as I slept to and fro.
The flu is a poor bed fellow, that's for sure;
But a bed, blanket and pillow help with the cure.

May 6, 2007

Throw That Pain

Throw that pain over your shoulder,
Bury that ache beneath a boulder.

Smile at problems out of the blue,
Tackle them with God, who does love you.

He has promised to be always near;
His nearness helps us conquer fear.

Each year we get nearer to that door;
Go through it with faith to life evermore.

September 2003

Time To Meditate

Time to meditate and to pray;
This is needful for us each day.
It is also a matter of the will,
Daily time set our heart to fill.

Aimless one, work at it really well,
It is not so easy to tell.
The Scriptures are all waiting there,
They go good with sincere prayer.

It is a game we must live,
Be ready to serve and to give.
Otherwise, we get to living slipshod,
Then first place is not given to God.

Others can soon be sure to tell
When we are not living our devotions well.
One has to guard that precious time,
Else we will live in another clime.

November 28, 2007

Time To Tie It Up

Great God of all mankind,
I look to You today;
Trying to get hold of living
After going to You in prayer.

The evening is being wrapped up
Before we seek to rest,
Lots of sorting and getting order;
I welcome You, my great Guest.

We all keep believing and growing,
We "look in" to read Your Word;
You speak to me as we read,
Sometimes there's a whisper we've heard.

You need no special time
With us to make a connection,
You are always quite available
As we look in your direction!

We are guided by feeling and faith;
No words really have to be exchanged.
We just know You are near,
That often makes things be rearranged.

You are so wonderfully near,
We get "fired up" as grandpa does relate;
We believe it as you touch us,
And even more as you ring at our heart gate.

What fellowship is shared and lived!
Your nearness puts our heart to singing,
We give room for you to touch us,
Oh how we sense the bells of Heaven ringing.

November 13, 2007

To Our Amaryllis

Thank you, our dear friends,
For gracing our dining table.
Here you've been with us all along;
How is it you've been able?

Your gracious form, your lovely lines,
Your design is pure perfection;
The colors in each smiling face
Are to us, a great selection.

Those smiling faces, glowing bright,
Say "hello" without a word.
An inspiring greeting for the day
Your tender spirit we have heard.

There comes the midday, warm to hot,
But you stay smiling every minute;
Fresher than daisies, you're our lilies.
Our life? We're glad you're in it.

Later on when you have gone
And we sit alone without you,
Our memories will recall your queenly grace
And recapture the colors, every hue.

April 1999

To Paula

Numerous years have come and gone,
Since you first began to cry,
Your were about two weeks old, sweet baby,
When I came from Texas to say good bye.

From Bird City to Camp Anza, California,
I went to our departure port,
There my field hospital unit went by boat,
To the CBI Theater, a trip that wasn't short.

After two years of service over there,
We come flying home on a plane;
Having gone over before on a ship,
Coming home by air wasn't the same.

There seemed to be a hallowed joy,
About coming back home by air.
I had put the fact of my return,
Into God's hands with a prayer.

How grateful I came with nary a scar,
To take you, Paula, in my arms.
Right away we became great friends,
As you shared your childhood charms.

Now, I've flown away in another cause,
Seeking to share the Gospel's story,
Love divine we spread abroad,
Inviting people to share God's glory.

This task is the greatest ever shared,
Taking the love of Christ to the lives of all.
What love, what joy this mission brings,
As we accept His daring call.

Do pray for us as we still go,
From here to there forever so long;
We tire not in taking His promises,
As we share them with love and a song.

September 12, 2000

To Rest

Now I take me to our bed,
Thanking You, God, for love and bread.
We are pushed each day to the limit,
So much to try to get in it.

November 20, 2007

To Sing It

Thank you, Father, for this day, for this day;
Help me better to know you, better to know you;
That I do Your will, most yielded and still.

Help me Father, most gracious Father, most gracious Father,
To meet you in prayer both here and there, both here and there;
That I be Your servant helping others, helping others.

In His footsteps I would follow Him, I would follow Him,
Down the road of service, down the road of service,
To His honor and glory, to His honor and glory.

Amen; Amen.

July 1, 2007

Up At 2:00 a.m.

What are you doing here at two
When you retired at ten?
Oh, I had to rise to meet a need;
Then my finger itched for a pen.

God is very near at every hour,
He is the Guard who never sleeps;
One of our greatest blessings
Is that our lives trusted in Him, He keeps.

This whole adventure in living
Is founded in a close fellowship with Him.
Were it not for that ,my friends,
We could only depend on happenstance and whim.

The Founder, the Creator of all life
Is He who has shown His face.
We see it in our precious Savior,
The Revealer of His divine grace.

It does not end with a cross;
We are privileged to see an opened tomb.
This great fact thrills our every thought;
It was destined from Mary's womb.

And yet, far beyond the time Mary lived,
Our Creator and Father of us all,
Established the eternal fact of life everlasting;
Our faith scales high over death's wall.

And so before I go back to bed
To rest once more for a time,
I find those hours of rest are but a few,
Compared to that of eternal life sublime.

Should I just go to rest eternally,
Never to awake in my present state,
It would all be a part of His plan,
Whose love for us never does abate.

June 2007

VIM Team to Venecia

They came from the north on a plane
To visit the high school in Venecia.
There they were given the best of care,
Receiving the warm welcome of the assistencia.

There were twenty-six in all, counting the leader;
All pitched right in from arrival.
The enthusiasm was wonderful to see,
Old Man Time had to plead for survival.

Old walls came down while new ones appeared,
It was some of the best unity I have seen.
By afternoon, the outer walls were sailing upward,
The spirit was really sharp and keen.

The twenty workers became a real machine;
The gears meshed and went into fifth.
If one wasn't most careful, for sure,
He would be lost while changing the shift.

Holes in the floors for rebar began the divisions;
Then the mix and the block were laid;
It wasn't long before the block in a course
Began threatening to be as high as the head.

The gals and guys worked like a machine.
It was the best of a team at work.
This was compassion in action for young people;
New classrooms without a quirk or a jerk.

Tomorrow new students would be seated
In the desks aligned in each room.
The spirit of growth and new learning
Sends ignorance and unlearning to doom.

Now we must keep reaching out to others;
They, too, will join in the battle
To make literacy a real preoccupation,
Giving our best and making old ignorance rattle.

June 25, 2007

Volunteering Is Fun

The day's work is history;
What we did, is done.
Whether or not it met the foreman's scrutiny,
We know we had a lot of fun.

Some nails had their heads on wrong
So we saved them for the other side.
I explained how that was, to little Joe,
And his eyes crossed, then opened wide.

You see, we all are ready volunteers.
Some things we know, some things we don't;
But we don't let that bother us too much,
Stop volunteering - we won't!

Wait and See

Waiting upon the Living Lord
Can be a most precious delight.
Amid all the morning silence,
One discovers anew the gift of sight.

How many wonders are daily missed,
As we just keep speeding on our way;
In a hurry to accomplish one more thing,
Driven on to get there, come what may.

Time taken to be alone with our God
Pays dividends in how we do what we do.
While we continue on that daily march
His tender regard for all travelers may become ours, too.

Our love for God is a glorious thing
When it takes to its heart, our neighbor.
So much blessing can be spread abroad
When, together, we learn to love and labor.

One world we shout, undivided we stand!
God loves us all from every land.
Beyond these words may our actions go,
Creating world fellowship and helping it grow.

August 1, 2004

We Must Witness

We must write what we feel,
For others must be told of Thee,
So many have not heard the news,
That 'tis Thee Who sets us free.

Sets us free from shackles various,
Kept us mute for ever so long,
Leaving us tongue-tied and silent,
When in our hearts is Heaven's song.

There is joy and hope for everyday,
There is light for the longest night,
Though we are most blind in spirit,
'Tis Thee that gives us Thy new sight.

Most blurred gifts, now able to see,
My desire is to share Good News,
Thy gift of forgiveness and blessed joy,
Hope beyond the deepest, darkest blues.

You are light and life for all,
We are entrusted how to share,
In you is everlasting trust,
In your love, show how we care.

Though we all are given life by thee,
Though we walked along most carelessly,
We now have purpose and reason to live,
To make a difference thru our witness, joyously.

No more do we remain most mute,
Tongue-tied no longer for we talk;
We tell of Thy grace by our voices,
We share our witness as we walk.

There is no end to our witness,
It is our joy to make Thee known,
Thy love sufficient for each day,
Your cross makes us your own.

February 21, 2007

We Ponder

But why shouldn't it happen this way?
God is in control, and in His time,
He's ready to bring in as He will,
His great salvation for all, sublime.

For you and me it seems a bit rare,
He comes in the form of the lowest low,
That the highest of high might reveal itself,
In a love that all can know.

This love is one that's beyond all else,
It's from the heart of the Creator of all life,
There is none else that can be so great,
Ending between God and man, the meaningless strife.

Written a long time ago

Weather We Get, Weather We Got

What's it going to do tomorrow?
It has rained all day today.
It has been a two-week rainy period,
Maybe it's no longer to stay.

Time and again we were caught
While going from one building to another;
The clouds just up and began to cry,
And did we ever get wet, yes my brother!

It sorta became a game today,
To see how much we could get done.
In between the showers we worked outside,
Then under cover, the victory was won.

However, almost everyone of us
Sooner or later became soaked.
It was then we all felt like the frogs;
As we greeted each other, we croaked.

At last we were able to call it a day,
And decided to let it do as it wished.
No one was surprised again,
As we accepted what it dished.

Still, still as a mouse it is,
Not a sound, not a drop or a drip;
Maybe it has decided to stop,
Then wait until the next trip.

All things work together for good
As we learn to accept it with joy.
The weather as it wishes to come,
Learning to be flexible, our energy to employ.

God, I thank you for making me, me;
You knew what it was I might could be,
You have helped me at every turn of the road,
It has been Your help when too heavy was the load.

You've kept me faithful at every new task,
It has been trying at times to wear no mask.
I've always wanted to be fair and true;
It matters not so much at what I'd do.

It helped me to be in a worthwhile place
And doing a job where I could keep pace.

November 17, 2007

Welcome Canyon, Texas Team

How good it is to see again,
That Canyon City, Texas, group,
To have them here to work again,
And sit down for a bowl of soup.

Many a mother in El Mirador,
Will bless their presence this year,
The children will play and laugh and sing,
And when departure comes, down drops the tear.

Hope springs up again for sure,
When some things are torn down,
Because it means a new house built,
And a new spirit comes to town.

Together they work and worship too,
They all welcome each new day,
Real joy springs up in fellowship,
More precious is He as they pray.

2007

We've Come – No End

Lord, we've come to the field,
We came to help the yield,
Sharing the Gospel of good cheer;
We found you already here.

Here your name is glorified,
Many hearts come, opened wide,
You fill them with your power,
They praise you by the hour.

Oh yes, you're on the field,
You're bringing an increasing yield;
More people have a new heart,
Now, they really do their part.

There shall be no end to this,
It ever leads to eternal bliss,
We come and go in His name.
Costa Rica will never be the same.

We've Come To Work

Tonight is the time to pack up again,
A time once more to say good bye.
There are some last words to say,
Then at last there is a long sigh.

How can you explain what it's like
To be at work for children and others;
House-building of different sorts,
In it we grow closer as sisters and brothers.

There comes time for daily Bible School,
Time for singing and praying well.
There is the experience of playing together,
The teachers have their stories to tell.

There may be some discussion daily,
A time when the children feel free to share.
They may ask questions really important;
In the interchange, they find we all care.

There is always time for refreshments,
A cool soft drink, a choice of flavor,
On a real warm day how it does satisfy,
A little like the refreshing joy of our Savior.

The time to go comes before we know it.
We've gotten so absorbed in each day's joy
That we enter into the whole program;
We freely feel at home, boy oh boy!

The new house begun in a rush
Really was advanced every day.
The group put their best into the task,
The next team will go all the way.

Some painted high on the roof,
Others put up divisions inside.
Still others worked, finishing on a floor.
Those outside, the sun almost fried.

The six little kids and the baby in bed
Welcomed us all ,with their mother.
With a well-advanced beginning –
The next team will finish it altogether.

February 2006

What and Where

What can you do to help others?
You can join a work team of sisters and brothers.
Where can you go to a beautiful land?
You can go to Costa Rica, it's really grand.

There you can see beauty all over the place,
There you will find people of most every race.
These Ticos are a most friendly lot,
Going there to work is your best shot.

When it gets too hot, we'll call up a cloud.
When it rains too much, we'll still be proud.
The rice and chicken will take a prize,
While "the pinto" for breakfast can be any size.

Here the people are friendly with good taste,
You'll see beautiful children, and parents with real grace.
They will love you and respect your presence;
Their neighborly manners are of real essence.

The Methodist church is growing with help from people like you;
The love of the Father is evident, every day anew.
Let us look to Him together and plan,
We will join our forces and do all we can.

When it comes time for us to part
We'll hold each other secure in our hearts.

Los Chiles, Costa Rica (Norte)
June 14, 2005

What Do You Do?

What do you do when there is more to do
Than you can ever get done in a day?
I guess you just have to do what you can,
And leave the rest in the hands of God, as you pray.

Next day will still be there for a new start,
Once again you may give it your best try.
Each day will be glad to receive all your best.
As you keep your aims and expectations high.

It's not only what you believe that's important,
It's also what you really "be."
We can recite our creeds and say our prayers,
But Christian love in action is the key.

Sometimes to help others get it right
You have to <u>be</u> it, right by their side.
Patience, love, and concern do help,
Also, the cheerful spirit and a smile ever so wide.

It helps for some to just be held,
To have a back rub for a time or two;
That just helps the weariness go away.
Relaxation is a needed gift for me and you.

Meditation often goes well with relaxation;
Being still and letting our Creator Father speak.
He doesn't have to say a single word,
But we get the needed message we seek.

It's that fellowship with the Father,
It's that gentle message from the Divine,
That feeds our souls, giving us strength,
Real living faith that is yours and mine.

I went to a sunflower field;
There planted in perfect row after row,
Millions of shining faces shone brightly,
Smiling faces were asking, "Do you know what we know?"

Back from Los Chiles, 2:00 a.m.
February 9, 2007

What Of Good Before I Sleep

Before I lay me down to sleep,
On this day's life, I take a peek.
What of good for God have I done;
Have I helped another "nobody" on the run?

Do I present a winsome life,
One that's gotten rid of inner strife?
Is the Living Master my real guide,
As I let my faith reach out worldwide?

Without Him at the center of my being,
I'm just a blind man, never seeing.
But with Him risen, living in me,
I'm able to present Him for others to see.

His love for them, too, will win the day,
And they, too, will follow in His way.
When love is shared and faith is shown,
Others will choose Him as their own.

Savior of all, Jesus is His name.
His touch on you, leaves you never the same.
Living in you, He's your light,
You can testify with all your might.

When each day is done, as is this day,
It's natural to look to Him and pray.
Then you can go and fall in bed,
Thankful for a place to lay your head.

2007

What Remedy?

I got up in the morning
With aerobics on my mind.
I looked for real determination –
None of that could I find.

Our house does not for us provide
A plan for exercise and stretching.
I've gotta make me a place
To stop this awful wretching.

What is wretching, do you ask?
Well, it's not feeling at your best.
You're aching and hurting from uptightness,
In most bone, mind, and muscle tests.

You are feeling you don't measure up,
You can't seem to break the weight cycle;
So you're up and down with diets,
You need more than just a bicycle.

So I'm going to get at it right,
Make me a place to exercise;
Get out and walk, and walk some more,
I hope this will be really wise.

But with my kind of aches, I fear,
It is more need of joint replacement.
I'm glad we don't have one –
Or I would have trouble climbing out of the basement.

May 5, 2008

What Wonder

Oh God and Father, what hast thou done,
In the giving of your only Son;
Sending love that gives itself on the cross,
And battles with death till the victory is won?

In it all you dare to promise us,
That as you whisper to us, our name,
You show us a love coming from above,
That helps us never to be the same.

We find ourselves as we follow Him,
And seek to walk in the ways He walks;
To find our strength coming from God,
As we talk to Him, like He talks.

Written a long time ago

When Healing Comes

Oh, those rascal leg cramps again,
Old over-worked muscles mistreated!
They can't do other than complain
'Ere the day's mission is completed.

What joy at last when day is done;
But again in the wee hours of the morning
After the medications have been applied,
During dreams they return all "a storming."

Good massaging almost does the trick,
Yet such efforts done while sleeping
Hardly answers the needs of aged muscles;
Their relief to them comes "a creeping."

After all, they scream their complaints,
These long days are too much for us;
We've stayed at it as long as possible,
But we just can't do other than fuss.

So at last ,with legs up and elevated,
Toes keeping rhythm in the air,
One almost drops back to sleep
While gentle treatment gives what's fair.

There comes the time after some petting,
When one almost returns to sleep;
Real recovery with satisfaction
Comes rejoicing at a creep.

Oh what joy returns with healing,
With that ointment working wonders;
What do you know? It's done again,
Healing comes to one while he slumbers.

Once again, one learns the lesson,
Easy does it if you expect to heal,
Too rapid and too strong the treatment
Does not let those leg muscles gladly feel.

November 5, 2007

With Him in the Morning

Thy morning is ever so still,
Hardly a bird is on the wing;
They, too, are silent before Thee,
Time to be still and not to sing.

Singing can come later with joy,
We must wait for our overflowing cup.
God in His gracious love is here,
Of His blessed feast do we sup.

We need begin no new morning alone,
With Him we start each new day;
His gentle power invades our being,
With thanksgiving, we bow our heads and pray.

It is good first just to listen,
To feel Him near, to sense His love,.
He comes to us, yet He is ever near;
We need not try to scale the heights above.

As He has promised so He fulfills,
"I will never leave you nor forsake you;"
I am with you both night and day,
Just reach out to me and find it's true.

With Tender Touch

Dear Lord of the tender touch,
You have blessed us all today.
Been with us as we share,
Led us in what to say.

You opened our hearts in love,
Gave us assurance as we spoke.
Lifted our confidence all day long,
Gave us fellowship with humble folk.

There were those who wondered "if."
Doubts lingered in our midst.
You gave us patience with them all,
Granted us the Spirit beyond the gist.

You helped us get out of the way
So others could Christ in us see.
Not in any way could we boast,
Except of your love, so full and free.

Sometimes when we are afraid to talk
Lest we be ashamed of what we say,
The Spirit nudges us onward
To share with others on the way.

For if we do not show and tell,
Limited will be the witness.
We're called to let Him live in us,
Make God's Kingdom be our business.

So let us speak beyond the mumbling,
Let us feel free in word and deed.
Let His message speak thru our living,
As when we help those in need.

When others lend a helping hand,
When they ask what they can do,
Be with us in all our teaching,
To share your example, clear and true.

August 3, 2004

Workers and Coworkers

No sir, man, there's no new birth;
You're of this world, bound to this earth.

By my God's the Maker of this universe,
Through His Son we're freed from the curse.

Oh yes, there is and from above,
There's a New World, one of love.

God came to redeem us all,
His love, His love lifts us from the fall.

And in His image we're created too,
With His guidance there is much we can do.

With His creativity in our souls,
We're coworkers with Him 'til our bell tolls.

New ways, a new world comes into view,
Let's get going, get at it, me and you.

Yes, let's get going to it, not just stand there.
God spoke to us this morning, near.

Jesus said, "My Father works unto now,"
Come on men, He'll show us how.

Jesus also said, "And I also work."
So let's get movin', there's no time to shirk.

You Have to Lay it on the Line

If there is ever going to be the Kingdom,
His kingdom of love ever so fine;
We must learn to be outgoing,
To lay our lives there on the line.

There will always be more yet to do,
When each day's work is done;
We're called to go the second mile,
If His victory is to be won.

It's on His road of dedicated service,
It's humility that shows the way,
His self-giving love is the answer,
Lived throughout each live long day.

Christians, we are called to be ever giving,
Be slow to say "This is mine."
Rather to share at His open table,
Invite each and everyone to dine.

There is no time to retire of faith,
The Kingdom offers all new wine,
All must go to invite the outcast,
And lay our lives there on the line.

We've no other way to do it,
Love builds the Kingdom of God;
It changes crosses into rolled-away stones,
Sends us to walk where He has trod.

May 9, 2007

Your Presence

Alone with Thee is this early hour;
Nothing to disturb a little time together.
Your day is awakening in the East;
You are available in all kinds of weather.

How wonderful it is to know for sure
That when we come to you, reaching up,
We find you already reaching down,
And present, to fill our empty cup.

Your Son reminded His disciples often
That your concern is for everyone.
There is no love like unto yours;
Your goodwill for all is never, never done.

Your concern for your great creation
Is perfect, regardless of what hour.
Eternal is your desire for the best;
Your love for every creature never loses power.

Though we behave like simple-minded things,
As careless in our ways as silly senseless sheep,
Your hand is still outstretched toward us
To catch us 'ere we fall, and into your safety keep.

Even when we insist in having our own way,
When we end up in the mire or broken on a shelf;
You are there to dress up whatever wounds,
To remind us we all need to look beyond ourself.

You have made us for close fellowship with you,
In this great universe given as our home.
We are of all creatures, the ones most stupid,
When from your loving presence, we insist to roam.

So Lord, turn on the switch in every heart;
Remind us that we are creatures of your hand,
Made to walk this earth in love and dignity;
Each day to sense your leading, as before you we stand.

So Good Morning, Heavenly Father, greetings from us to you.
You are ever present as we rise another day.
Your presence fills our eager waiting spirits
While we look heavenward, to stand or kneel to pray.

August 8, 2005

A Ewe and Her Lamb

By chance I was in the Inn Keeper's shed;
Its roof was a topping for a dugout cave.
With me was my newborn lamb that night;
We had been chosen as the two to save.

Others had been sent to pasture or for offerings;
The temple celebrations demanded many of our kind.
How glad I was that we were spared;
Now for another year I could have peace of mind.

We had found us a place in a corner;
There we would lie down for the night.
We expected no one else to appear
Until the dark gave way to morning light.

We only half awakened at the sound
Of others coming to look for this stable.
They came weary and worn, looking for rest,
And soon were settled as they were able.

Wondering who they were, I there awakened
When there were sounds of humans, restless.
Something special seemed to be taking place;
Was someone ill, needy, or in distress?

Shortly though I realized, as I heard a cry,
A cry from a newborn - this we mothers know.
How with flickering candlelight I saw
'Twas the birth of a baby, with a mother's voice low.

She was singing a sweet, tender lullaby
As her newborn took his first meal of milk.
Who were they that they should come here?
They were common folk for sure, nothing of silk.

My little one behaved real well and slept;
It was I, who could look and wonder.
That night as well, others came, all excited;
They had come from the hills over yonder.

It is not given to us to know many things;
Yet, there was in my heart the feel of belonging.
I seemed to feel that one day I should know
That this newborn child would heal much wronging.

He would be a really good Shepherd;
He would look for those who are lost.
He would save them all, everyone.
He would do it, no matter to Him the cost.

A Little Gray Mouse

There was a little gray mouse, on that special night,
When a new little baby was born, as a star shone bright.
The mother's name was Mary; the little mouse saw it all;
It blinked and scampered 'round in that stable stall.

In the stall there was a manger full of fresh hay;
It was there that Mary put newborn Jesus to lay.
Of course, she also took Him in her arms to coo;
She gently held Him, nursed Him, humming a song or two.

She was surprised by the shepherds who came from the hills;
They shared what had happened – Mary's heart leapt with thrills.
She knew all over again she was a chosen vessel;
She was not day dreaming with doubt, no need to wrestle.

So on that night, after all shared their very own story,
They were convinced that God had shared His glory.
The shepherds left the stable, praising God all the way;
They shared what had happened – God had come to stay!

The little gray mouse continued to run all around;
Mary and Joseph had packed up and left for new ground.
He just couldn't quite figure out what it was all about.
Why, he missed that family so much, he wanted to shout!

And aren't we like that little mouse watching?
We see and feel His very Presence coming,
We are privileged to be a part of God's revolution.
We want to share with others the real solution.

December 15, 2005

A Little Puppy Shares

A little puppy slept in the stall,
And awakened when Jesus was born.
No one like this had shared his home;
Now he would always feel less forlorn.

He had found this place one cold night
When he was shooed away from the inn.
They, too, had no room for him there;
He was a homely sight, most thin.

He had lost his mother when they moved,
For there were also street dogs then.
And no one much seemed to care
Where new litters were going, or had been.

He had stopped to rest while the others ate
What the lady had thrown out the door.
When he awakened, lo and behold!
The rest of the family wasn't there anymore.

What to do he did not know the least;
He just kept going half tumbling along.
The rays of light that beckoned from a door
Gave hope as he heard both music and song.

Half running there to inspect the sight,
He found instead a crust of bread and went away.
Following other animal smells, he padded along
To find a cave shed with some hay.

The cave shed became for him a home;
The caretaker gave him a squirt or two of milk.
After eating what he found thrown from the inn,
His bed of hay this time seemed as soft as silk.

But then, it was a lonesome way to live;
There wasn't much new to meet the eye.
Until this one special night with a new event,
When a couple came to utter a thankful sigh.

They were oh, so weary, all three of them -
The donkey, the man, the lady great with child.
The man cared for her well, but in the night
Things really happened fast and wild.

With mere candle light that flickered,
The man was new at his task.
It was all very real – the moans and the groans;
Neither of them was hiding with a mask.

This was a normal child-bearing time,
But in a tiny, most humble place.
The baby finally let out a squall,
As He came to live among the human race.

I don't know who had counseled the mother,
Most a teenager she was and fair.
She did so well in the humble surroundings;
Her child would have the best of care.

When things were almost settled down,
The child had nursed and we needed rest.
Excited shouts and voices filled the air;
It turned into a sharing time most blest.

The shepherds of the hills told what they saw;
They shared the messages given and sung.
The mother's heart beat fast as she shared, too;
She and Joseph knew now God's plan had begun.

God had been at work as He had promised;
Heaven was bending low with Eternal Love.
The Baby was born to be the Savior of all,
As the angels sang in unison above.

How do I know this? Well, you see,
I was lost and had no home at all.
The same God who helps you become unlost
Is the One who led me to this stall.

If I could sing, I would every day,
And I would share as those shepherds did.
I would help God turn over every living soul,
Flush them all out wherever they've hid.

I'm just one lost member of a large litter in Bethlehem,
Who found a home far into the night.
Now I've seen what the Maker of the stars
Is doing to help everything turn out right.

I believe love like this is unbeatable;
Only God Eternal could so love a lost world.
Only He would give of His best treasure.
Only God spreads His love unfurled.

A Sparrow's Viewpoint

I'm but a little sparrow!
My Heavenly Father feeds me well.
To fly and sing and eat His seeds
Is a blessing, I'm here to tell.

I cannot sing like other feathered brothers,
But I can chirp and flit with glee.
I sometimes become a bother, I know;
And when that happens, it troubles me.

You know I've a story to tell to my kin,
Because great has been my joy.
One night I awakened with half an eye
And saw the birth of a special little Boy.

From my ringside seat in the stable,
I heard his first strong cry.
How tenderly his young mother held him!
You could feel it! My, oh my, oh my!

There watched close by a devoted man,
Who was at the mother's beck and call.
Shepherds came running from the hills!
Yes siree, I saw and heard it all!

I have a big feeling in my little heart,
Which I'm going to pass along to others.
I feel some day when this Baby is a Man;
He'll tell people that we sparrows are their brothers!

For we all know that we are loved,
All of us, small and large, short and tall.
Daily we see how God provides for us.
He's our Creator and the Savior of us all.

So you remember now that a little bird
Rejoiced on that special Holy night.
When Jesus was born I learned his name;
And oh, how precious was the sight!

Answers

Oh God, how easily each generation forgets
That only you are the Lord of all.
You it is, on whom the life of people depends,
You only have the answer for our fall.

We cannot of ourselves find the answers
To our questions of life, death, and worth.
It took You to send your loveliest Gift;
"Forgiving love" begun in a Holy Baby's birth.

Christmas 1997

At Christmas

What seek you in this season
When the Christ Child experienced birth?
Do you sense the labor of centuries;
God at work to reveal our worth?

Come to save us from our sin;
Prophets promised His coming sure.
He teaches all who will listen
How each life can become really pure.

To seek the oneness with the Father,
Full submission becomes the way.
Self-sacrifice, the road to redemption;
Union with the Father through each day.

Just think how the cross and resurrection
Become God's way, the Scriptures say,
To bring to us our Salvation.
It all began in a manger of hay!

May 2008

Candles

Candle, Candle, burning bright!
How did you glow on that night?
There was no other to assist, I say;
Joseph helped sweet Mary where she lay.

Normal birth it was, without a flaw;
No innerspring mattress, just new straw.
Animals witnessed that humble birth;
Jesus came as Savior of all the earth.

Simply wrapped in plain swaddling tog;
His little face left the shepherds agog.
Seldom did he just up and cry;
He shared little more than a simple sigh.

A little Baby – to cancel the debt of sin;
A crucified Savior – to bring the Kingdom in.
Maybe it was not all done within the law,
But it was the greatest love man ever saw.

The lowly manger becomes a Holy place;
The cruel cross, the sign of God's grace.
Those who saw went out to tell;
The shepherds and disciples did many things well.

Now you and I, as candles glow,
The love of Jesus, in our faces show.
And while we seek to tell the glad news,
God makes others ready our Lord to choose.

Celebrating Christmas

I've been wondering, you know,
For it seems to me quite queer;
From most of what is going on
With what I can see and hear;

Folk seem to say one thing;
Then turn around to do the other,
Not meaning to do what they say;
Why do they take all that bother?

Let's make some changes, my brethren;
Let's put Jesus in first place.
Let's help others rejoice at His name;
Let's put a smile on each face.

Come, give, to help good tidings
Reach to those who haven't heard.
Look, we can pool our resources
To prepare one called to preach the Word.

Have you ever thought how it would please Him,
If on the day that is His birthday,
We would be helping others to praise and serve Him,
While He walks with us all the way?

Now, we're not trying to be a "fuddy-duddy,"
Nor are we trying to be a sour "kill-joy;"
We're just saying, let's cease being hypocrites
And take seriously the means we employ.

November 20, 2007

Christmas

Teenage Mary listens to an angel from the sky;
She's given a promise, she accepts with a sigh.
Later she sings, as the baby inside her grows;
She's amazed from her head to the tips of her toes.

She's keen on the message that she received;
"She's to be the mother of the Messiah," this she believed.
The coming of this baby, by her to be born,
Shall change the world that's all tattered and torn.

And it's about changing the lives of all people, too.
Jesus shall make a difference in all that they do.
The high shall become lowly, and the lowly, become high.
World-wide changes shall come – this Child is why.

Prophets with visions, write with keen foresight;
Angels come singing in the sky at night.
Shepherds listen to the message in their humble sheepfold;
They run to see if the truth to them's been told.

They race to find the baby that's born in a stall;
Can it be true that He's come, the Savior of all?
They find the baby fast asleep in young Mary's arms,
And Joseph keeping them safe from all possible harms.

Mary tells her story of what's come to pass;
All that's happened to her while being merely a lass.
The shepherds tell Mary of the heavenly choir and the song;
What the angel said they'd find, if they'd just hurry along.

So they shared, all amazed, thrilled from the start;
Mary took it all in, and hid it all in her heart.
The shepherds lingered a bit, then went back;
Having Good News for the whole world, so none would lack.

November 20, 2006

Christmas and Gift-Giving

I asked myself about Christmas
And its real meaning for me.
Is there more in it than gift-giving?
What more is there in it for me to see?

While making my list of the obligated ones,
Those that I just really have to give,
Someone said that Christmas is a discovery;
It's about finding a new way to live.

They said it's about what God has done
To bring people closer to His side.
And that what He did in wee little Bethlehem,
He did for all people, far and wide.

It seems that He was really bothered
About the rebellion found in everyone's heart;
About the desire to be the emperor in one's own life,
And that right from the very start.

Rebellion buys suffering, so much pain and hurt;
It keeps spreading everywhere, year after year.
So He still offers Christmas with love,
To dispel the terror, the hate, and the fear.

Christmas is not about gift-giving only;
It's about finding a new way to live.
It's not about asking, "What do I get?"
Rather is to ask, "What's the best I can give?"

It's finding that the Baby born in the manger
Grew to be a youth, and a man as God's son.
He gave His life on the cross to save us all;
Faith in Him begins a new life for everyone.

December 2, 1998

Christmas Must Be More

Christmas may be formed of tinsel and lights;
It, however, must be more of His in Heaven bright.
Gifts may be given by both the rich and the poor,
But He's the best gift; the Baby Jesus means life forever more.

Candles and choral singing, even "The First Noel,"
The message of gladness, we all know it well,
Peace on earth I give you and to all my goodwill,
In my Son is my love, sent from Heaven's windowsill.

We may, like some, begin with a real early start,
But that is one of commercialism's greatest sins, 'tis sure.
Get what you can no matter the way, the cost;
God's gift is lost in the melee of celebration impure.

Better to take a candle and in a closet closed,
Or go out on a hillside, alone with a heavenly sight,
Seek the presence of Almighty God by candle light,
And sense His wondrous love, coming by starlight.

And then to realize that God is ever present;
He is taking care of His creation everywhere.
He is speaking to us always, asking us, saying,
Be ye, too, with me, real caretaker, sharing love as you can.

May 7, 2008

Christmas Time

Oh God, may we at this Christmas time,
Take time to listen – take time to see.
May we close no door to Your entrance;
May we keep our hearts wide open to Thee.

Even as Joseph and Mary asked for a room,
A place to give birth to the King of the Universe,
Jesus still asks to be born in our lives.
May we not send Him to a smelly stable – or worse!

May we really and truly take time for Thee;
Stop our running long enough to hear the rush of angels' wings.
To run to the stable to see Thy majesty displayed
In the arms of a teenager, Thy Son, her baby, to whom she sings.

Help us, Father, to keep your Son in Christmas;
You are the Author of this special day.
We are not ruled by silly laws of prevention;
Christmas is the birthday of the world's Savior – it's His day.

Let the supermarkets and business places
Fail to recognize it in their greeting.
We Christians will declare, "Merry Christmas!" always!
It's the special day when God and man are meeting.

God is still seeking to help each new generation
Be in real fellowship with Him every livelong day.
All habitation needs to recognize His majesty;
The living God is revealing His love always!
He is here to stay!

December 18, 2005

Christmas With Love

I asked myself about Christmas,
And it's real meaning for me.
"Is there more in it than gift giving?"
"What more is there for me to see?"

While making my list of the obligated ones,
Those to whom I just really have to give.
Someone said that Christmas is a discovery;
It's about finding a new way to live.

They said it's about what God has done
To bring people closer to His side,
And that what He did in wee little Belén
He did for all people far and wide.

It seems that He was really bothered
About the rebellion in everyone's heart;
About the desire to be the Emperor in one's life,
And that right from the very start.

Rebellion brings suffering, so much pain and hurt;
It keeps spreading everywhere year after year.
So He still offers Christmas with love
To dispel the terror, the hate, and the fear.

Christmas is not about gift-giving only,
It's about finding a new way to live.
It's not about asking, "What do I get?"
Rather, in love, asking, "What's the best I can give?"

It's finding that the baby born in the manger
Grew to be a youth and a man as God's son.
He gave His life on the cross to save us all,
Faith in Him begins a New Life for everyone!

December 2, 1998

Come to the Manger

From how far had they come
Before they were refused at the Inn?
Journey worn, both man and beast,
Little impression made on the village dim.

Care and rest was their great need,
Really time to be all alone.
In the "fullness of time," Oh, it is here!
Heaven would attest as the stars shone.

Though there was no regular space,
They found a stable, a cave-like shed.
This would do for the Creator's Son
Anywhere he could lay down his head.

Later, He would share with everyone,
The rich, the poor, the lost, the last and the least.
His love, once given room in the heart,
Would grow and grow as Heavenly yeast.

"Thy kingdom come, Thy will be done,"
This theme He would teach.
God's Kingdom, both without and within,
Cancels sin's grasp by love's reach.

Oh, what glory came that night!
What miracle happened in that shed!
Mary gave birth to little Jesus.
In that lowly manger she laid down His head.

It's never very far to that shed;
Everyone is welcomed at the stall.
It just takes a silent, opened heart
To give time to the Spirit's call.

Let's take time to pause and to listen.
We, too, can hear the angels sing.
Peace on Earth, Goodwill to men!
Glory to God, let the Heavens ring!

December 24, 2002

Dear Santa Claus

Oh, S.C.
Dear Santa Claus,
Your beard's so long and very white.

Oh, S.C.
Dear Santa Claus,
I must admit, you're quite a sight.

You only come but once a year
But when you come......

You bring good cheer.

2005

Drummer Boy

You can sing about the drummer boy,
Who played his drum for the Christ Child.
We can sing along with another drummer boy,
Who fairly bounces as he run-runs wild.

He cannot be more than twelve years old,
Like Jesus was, with the doctors in the temple.
He's so full of music, it has to show,
It's just all that pure and simple.

He's in command right where he sits,
Of that there's no doubt at all.
It's a sight to see as you laugh and cry;
He for sure has heard God's call.

The Lord, the Giver of talents and power,
Speaks through this boy for sure.
We give Him thanks for His loving grace
As He makes Johnny's world endure.

Christmas Eve 2002

Eternal Answer Source

Oh God, how easily each generation forgets
That only you are the Lord of all.
You it is on whom the life of people depends;
You only, have the answer for our fall.

We cannot of ourselves find the answers
To our questions of life, death, and worth.
It took You to send your loveliest gift
"Forgiving love" begun in a Holy Baby's birth.

Christmas 1997

Go to Bethlehem

Go to Bethlehem, go right away!
There in a stable with fresh hay,

You will find the baby,
And I don't mean maybe.

He'll be all wrapped up well.
Listen! His mother has a story to tell.

This whole story is a continued one;
Many chapters are yet to be done.

Run now in haste and go there;
You'll find a couple showing loving care.

Listen well to all her words;
Tell her I have sent you and all you've heard.

When you leave them, share with all
What you've seen and heard, to witness well.

December 21, 2001

God Made Christmas

I turned my eyes to the cradle
In a manger in little Bethlehem.
There I found God making Christmas,
As He sent His Son back then.

They all were real, willing characters,
Though Joseph needed a nudge or two;
Mary and the humble rustic shepherds,
Wise men, with their camels a few.

Self-important doctors and old King Herod
Are found in the world each year.
They fail to see the angel;
The meaning of the message, they don't hear.

The meek, the lowly, and the needy
Receive His love from the start.
God answers the most sincere desires
Of every open and humble heart.

Have You

Have you ever thought what it means to Jesus,
As He observes how we celebrate His birthday?
How pleased He is if He finds us rejoicing,
And helping others be thankful as they pray.

Let us help people see the purposes of God,
As we share redemption's story,
God's interest shown in each and every person,
As He wrapped up His love in His Son, Mary's boy.

Let us tell it as it was at the First Christmas,
The sincerity of Mary's acceptance and her boy,
As God chose her to be the vessel for His Son,
The child to be the world's Savior <u>is her</u> boy.

November 20, 2007

Have You Ever Thought

Have you ever thought how much it might please Jesus,
If on the day that is His birthday,
We would be helping others rejoice and praise Him,
While He walks with us all the way?

Now, we're not trying to be difficult,
Nor are we trying to be a "kill-joy."
We are just saying, let's cease being hypocrites,
Let's take seriously the means we employ.

Let's help people see the tremendously deep meaning
Of God's action in showing the whole story;
The interest He had, and has in us all, everyone –
As he wrapped up His love in His Son, Mary's little boy.

Let's tell it as it was at the First Christmas,
The sincerity of Mary's acceptance and joy;
At being chosen as the vessel to bear His Son,
The Child to be the Savior of the world is her boy.

October 2007

He Has Come, He is Here

An angel in a starlit sky,
Shepherds out on a hill.
A baby lay in a manger,
A mother waiting still.

A little boy with a lamb,
A donkey in the stall,
Joseph standing close on guard,
Ready to protect them all.

The bright shining star in the East,
The wise men on camels slow,
Riding long by day and night,
Started, they onward go.

The bright star, one night stands still;
The wise men find the mother and child.
As they bring their suitable gifts,
Mary's heart keeps beating wild.

The hours too quickly pass away;
The wise men rise to go –
They now return by another route,
On their camels, tall and slow.

Many centuries even now have passed.
Have we found the Holy Child?
Have you given Him your life?
Is your heart also beating wild?

Oh dear God, come to this world,
Enter every beating heart.
We wait for you, we love you too!
Come enter our hearts and never depart.

"Oh, silly child," you say to me,
I've already come to you in my Son.
Accept Him as your Savior, too.
Tell others 'til your work is done.

Heavenly Music!

Oh my, yes, there was music!
There was really something to sing about.
The heavens were filled full of music;
The angelic choir wanted fairly to shout.

There was not so much the heavy thunder type –
It was the fine, piercing, high-noted kind.
It came from on high and over the hills;
It spoke to the soul, and also to the mind.

The overpowering type would have bothered the child;
Mary's gentle spirit needed something fine.
Here she was, obeying the message given her;
She needed to be reassured, "You and He are mine!"

Assured she was, along with Joseph watching there,
As the shepherds told of what came to them high over the hills.
They seemed still to be hearing as they listened –
Their faces fairly shone, stirred by the Spirit that thrills.

Used to being alone at times, awake and listening,
The safety of the sheepfold, always on their mind,
They remembered the angelic voices singing.
Now they listened, at attention, fixed, as though blind.

They would speak and share when asked;
They shared how they seemed heaven sent.
Thus the reason they came out of breath,
For they had come, arriving breathless and spent.

Only now, after listening to Mary's words of sharing,
Mixed with her deep-filled words of gratitude,
Did they go to share everywhere what had occurred.
They felt sent now to share with firm attitude.

December 2007

"Here Comes Santa Claus!"

Today, I'm going to be Santa Claus!

I'm to be with the little ones in a school!

Help me, Lord, to use this opportunity.

I want to tell them of Jesus.

I'm your tool!

December 17, 2007

His Day

Santa Claus, decorated trees, perfect lighting,

Have nothing really serious to say.

The tremendous meaning of Christmas

Is seen in the manger.

It's His day.

We tend to paganize the great Divine.

We rob the most Holy of His power

As we take advantage for our gain,

To make it become our own hour.

How Harried A Life

How harried a life we all live,
In our absorbing Christmas each year.
It's a happy season, a holiday's blessing;
Special shopping sales stand us on our ear.

Get there early or it'll be sold,
There aren't that many left.
The options overwhelm parent and child;
It's no wonder many at last, feel bereft.

Thankful am I that I'm so occupied,
That I've not time for all of that shopping.
It's better to be involved in making Him known;
In letting Him be first with no stopping.

Take time to read the whole story.
What was God doing, what was His plan?
He was showing his love for us in Jesus;
How better could we learn in one life's span?

By faith we take Him as He speaks;
He is as He says in His Word.
God has come to earth to save us;
It's the greatest true story we've ever heard.

Sing, oh ye believers, sing it loudly;
Some are most occupied, or cannot hear.
Share your joy, share it gladly,
Help another believe and cast out fear.

I Dare Believe It, I Pray!

In the manger lay the babe,
Nor was there crying for to hear.
There was but joyous hearts all beating;
Mary was so glad, she shed a tear.

How could it be that I be chosen
From all the others to be blest?
Oh my God, how great the wonder
To be the Mother amid the rest.

Take Thou me and make me able,
Help me 'neath each day's sky
To trust in Thy glorious wisdom –
Never again to ask Thee, "Why?"

Each day shall be to me a privilege,
Each night to lie, and with Him rest.
Great is this challenge set before me;
Make me able to do my best.

Thank you for your promise,
Thou art with me all the way.
Thy Child, Thy Son, oh gracious God,
I dare believe it, I dare, I pray.

Mary's son and God's son, too,
An open heart, a daring mind.
God acts as only He can do;
He comes to save us, ever kind.

2003

I Wonder

I wonder what Mary really thought
When there was no room in the Inn.
Did she wonder how it could be?
Did she feel her chances were growing thin?

So far had been the journey south,
Down from her far-away Galilee.
When would she return to her parents?
How could this uncertainty be?

But having been promised by the angel eternal,
That she would be given aid,
All was to work out in the harmony;
So down her baby she laid.

Now by the lowly manger light
She wrapped her newborn child,
While thoughts sped through her mind
And wonder raced her heart most wild.

"Fear not, unto you a child is born,"
"Unto you a son is given."
God's Kingdom is coming in!
Evil's hold on man is riven!

Prophesy this night is still being fulfilled
By this, her first child's birth.
Peace between God and man
Is now really come to Earth.

Having been told to go to Bethlehem,
We also come running to the manger
With our hopes amid our fears,
Love brings us amid the danger.

December 21, 2001

Israel Waited

Israel had waited, waited long,
But God had waited longer.
The disobedient had their idols worshiped;
The hope of the faithful grew ever stronger.

In the fullness of time God did speak
In the language of Eternal Love.
He sent His Son by a lowly maid,
His messenger appearing from above

Mary listened and gave herself;
The shepherds heard the song.
In due time she went to Bethlehem with Joseph,
And they came by donkey right along.

It happened as it was promised;
The baby lying in a manger.
God's gift for each and everyone;
The Savior would not be a stranger.

Have you, too, waited long?
Or have you made Jehovah wait?
Don't waste another single moment!
Open wide, wider still, your gate.

Go forth and tell it evermore –
Let no thing, no one, you detain.
Tell the Good News of God's love!
Preach it, teach it, live it again and again.

Dec 21, 2000

Just As They Had Been Told

The shepherds, out among the hills,
Were privileged on that night.
The heavenly chorus filled the skies;
The angels appeared in dazzling light.

The chorus sang of peace and goodwill;
God was sending His best to earth.
"Go to Bethlehem and look for Him,"
The angel declared His place of birth.

"Let's go and see if this is true,
In a manger we're to find the Child."
Could it be that they heard well?
They made haste with hearts beating wild.

Arriving there, "Lo, in a manger lay
The Baby wrapped in humble fare."
They shared their story, face opened wide
As Mary showed the Baby tender care.

So they shared and were amazed.
"Could He be the awaited Promised One?"
One thing for sure, the shepherds knew,
It was just as the angel said it would be done.

Now, lo, these many years gone by,
We, too, speed as they also sped.
Our hearts beat wild in our breasts
As to the manger we are led.

Oh, Little One, who became a child,
And later still became a man,
You love me, too, as you speak my name.
I come in faith as best I can.

You died for us upon that cross,
And God raised you from the tomb.
Eternal life you give to us,
Predestined Savior, from Mary's womb.

Little Angel Boy

What do you have to tell us,
You little angel boy?
Sent by God to whisper,
So many would your help employ.

Oh, the message isn't just for us.
It's really for them to hear!
Time will come for us to shout.
Time will come when we will cheer.

Time will come later when, with others,
You will come to make the heavens ring.
'Twill be with that heavenly chorus,
As you all Good Tidings bring.

December 16, 2004

Manger Danger

Lo, we spend these times of Christmas
In the glory of His manger,
Knowing full well now, as back yonder,
There is always the presence of danger.

Even then they sought to undo Him,
While He was yet a tiny child.
He escaped by way of Egypt;
Slain were others when fear ran wild.

Jealous Herod, ruling from His throne,
Ordered those many children slain.
Left were those Bethlehem mothers,
Racked in suffering and pain.

Terrorism rampant wherever, when,
Must be faced head-on, erased.
Evil, hatred, revenge, all are challenged.
As God's love is in hearts enclosed.

December 21, 2001

Mary What Did You Think?

Mary, what did you think when Joseph came?
He'd come back from the Inn; the news was the same.

"No room, no room, there's no room for you."
You thought, "But I've got to have a room, for the baby is due."

It was getting late and Joseph heard a noise –
Maybe back there a ways, or was it some boys?

Anyway, they went back and what they found
Was not a room or a porch, but a big hole in the ground!

It was a crude refuge for cattle and others –
It was a cave for animals, and especially for new mothers.

It gave shelter from the winds and the night's cold,
But there was hardly a clean place for a blanket to unfold.

You went to work, for there wasn't much time,
While Joseph cared for the donkey, humming a tune sublime.

Your pangs let you know as Joseph kept the fire,
That the baby was coming, as you began to perspire.

You helped yourself that night, as much as you could,
And Joseph was a blessing, so helpful and good.

When Jesus was clean and wrapped up well,
You knew even more, there was a story to tell.

The thoughts you had were given real proof,
As the shepherds came to see Jesus under your roof.

What great news they told of the angel and the choir,
And the message they heard of what would transpire.

They found, as promised, you and Joseph and the Christ Child.
And all of you shared, with your hearts racing wild.

What more was to come, what more could there be?
That would come in due time, you would have to wait and see.

But this we all know, it was a special night for you,
As you gave birth to Jesus and heard him coo.

May It Be Beautiful

Let this Christmas be pure delight,
Especially on His holy night.
Forget much of the commercial spree,
Unshake yourselves and be free.

Let meaningful carols fill the air,
Hymns of faith and wonder everywhere.
Prayers of thanksgiving, prayers of grace,
God has come in Jesus, to show His face.

Newborn Baby, both Savior and child,
Sets our hearts fairly racing wild.
Even for each of us He has come,
Oh glory, glory, Jesus, our voices hum.

Released from all sin's chains,
In our hearts the Savior reigns.
With this Christmas, God offers anew,
His very presence and power, too.

Child of promise, child of delight,
Born to save us on this night.
Lowly manger is Thy bed,
Pillow of hay to rest Thy head.

We bow before Thee, God's Holy Son,
And before you, Mighty Father, Thy will be done.
Christmas joy in our hearts each day,
Come, O come, and with us, stay.

December 7 & 8, 2003

Morning Has Come!

Morning has come. The day has broken.
The sun was bright in the east.
What happened to the early beauty?
It was swallowed by a foggy beast!

Marching up the valley without permission,
It came to take over our Christmas spirit;
But it shall have a challenge strong
From "The Light of the World," God's candle lit.

Little bitty baby born in a manger,
Cradled there by gentle Mary.
He will, one day, save the people;
Though it means a cross to carry.

How slow and stupid still are we;
Crazy, lewd fashions everywhere,
Stirring the passions all aflame,
Marching toward Hades, without a care.

December 19, 2006

My Lonely Vigil

While the loved ones sleep and rest,
I, my lonely vigil keep.
Was it like this on that Holy Night,
While the shepherds were guarding their sheep?

The Lord's angel came to stir those who slept;
His message was especially for their hearing.
The heavenly chorus, too, came to sing
On this night of the Messiah's appearing.

Long years had past; generations come and gone,
Yet the Promised One's coming lingered.
Now at last, while the needy world slept,
God's direction to the stable fingered.

For there was to be born, in lowly way,
Of a maiden of God's own choosing,
The Son of God, the battle to win;
E'en now the devil starts losing!

December 1997

Oh Dear God!

"Oh dear God, come to this world!

Enter every beating heart.

We wait for you, we love you.

Come to us and never depart."

"Oh silly child," I say to you,

"I've already come in my Son.

Accept Him as your Savior, too.

Tell others till His work is done."

Only a Few Days to Christmas

Only a few more days to Christmas!
Just like other times, many things yet undone.
Instead of just going through all the motions,
We're racing from here to there, on the run.

It's time to take the ears in hand, right firmly.
To ask some simple questions and to think,
"What relationship does most of what we're doing
Have to do with Jesus birth? Where's the link?

All this promotion, this pressure of buying and selling,
This idea that there needs to be a gift,
Has His coming, through God's marvelous love,
Renewed in us the need to help others have a lift?"

When we stop and take time to analyze it,
This desire to give and this need to receive,
We find, built within us one and all.
Why should it be so hard for us to run to the manger and believe?

We are talking about the God of the universe!
He has planned it and done it all so well.
We Christians are called to go, receive this baby gift,
And run from the manger, like the shepherds, to tell.

How we need the high gift of forgiveness.
How we need to all be washed clean.
Get shed of all our sins, our cares and sorrows,
Bow before Him and His love, hearing, "See what I mean.

This is my love, wrapped up in this Baby.
Follow Him as He grows to teach, to heal, and to save.
Look at his broken body on the cross freeing you.
Run, find everlasting life given back in the empty cave."

Go, share what you've found, feel, and believe.
Help others believe and come to know;
Go, work, share, help, preach, explain –
Time is short for us who dwell here below.

December 23, 2000

PUSHED!

Christmas is coming way too fast!

I'll be ready among the last!

Too much to do while on the go!

I can't get my gearshift out of low!

If I start now, perhaps by next year

I'll be ready, with reason to cheer.

December 21, 2006

Really Wild!

Go ye away, both sleep and slumber;
Leave me to write for Him.
Though this body may tire and give way,
My cup keeps flowing over the brim.

Just think, the Good Shepherd has come tonight;
He's sleeping in a manger, a newborn child.
I cannot take it all in, it is so vast;
Born in a manger, God's Son.

That's Really Wild!

December 1997

Salvation, A Wiggly Babe!

The Spirit swept over the shepherds and fold.
The wind brought cold to the small flock.
But fires would burn in the hearts of all,
Once they went to the cave made of rock.

'Twas there they would find at last
What God had promised for ages and ages.
Salvation for man, wrapped up in a Babe,
Good news on this page, of all pages.

Come to my cradle and look at me,
Come and I will give you a smile.
Though I am only a wiggly Babe,
I'm the One you've waited for all the while.

History made new and prophecy revealed;
It's more than the human mind can grasp.
It's true and I'm here, God's promise kept;
It causes even the most holy to gasp.

Yet before it's all said and really done,
Birth, the call, the cross and the tomb –
People will be reminded of the way God works.
His salvation comes by the Fruit of the womb.

The Author of all life knows no defeat;
His ways may not be the ways of man.
But His ways are right and eternally true;
What man is unable to do, He can!

December 1997

- S A N T A -
A Plane, a Whirlybird, a Jet???

Here I sit in my Santa suit,
Waiting patiently for the word.
I'm to go up to the guest house
Hearing the children's joy, greatest ever heard.

With a Ho, Ho, Ho and a Go, Go, Go,
I'll be walking up the road.
In Canada, Dancer's well-worn harness broke,
Now I hurry along with part of the load.

Those little eyes will watch every move;
Is this the real Santa we've read about?
Can it be that he's been sick?
He doesn't seem to have all the clout.

Maybe he's a "stand in" or something,
But his suit does seem to be real.
And his beard is real – not that cotton stuff;
He doesn't mind if you try to feel.

Yet he has a long way to go
If he's to get to everyone all around.
What's he going to do anyway,
If he spends this much time on the ground?

Oh well, maybe he has a plane or two;
Also, maybe a helicopter whirlybird.
Anyway, I'm not going to worry about him;
He'll be able to manage, if it's true what I've heard.

Oh well, I guess that's up to him.
Yes, maybe he has a plane or two.
If he does, it's going to have to be a jet –
Or someone's going to be missed, maybe you!!

Sharing God's Plan

The shepherds in the fields with their sheep
Were all prepared for a night of sleep.
All at once there was music in the sky.
Angelic voices began to come from on high.
The shepherds looked up with fear and awe;
They couldn't believe what their weary eyes saw.
The music and the words were ever so plain.
It told of praise to God and where a child was to be lain.
The shepherds listened well, and then ran to Bethlehem.
Obedient they were; no need to explain again.
They found the Child as they'd been told.
They listened and listened to God's plan unfold.
For Mary told her story, and Joseph added more
That thrilled all their hearts and evened up the score.
They were well within God's plan for man.
God was reaching down with promised salvation again.
The shepherds were but simple people of the field –
They had to trust more in God than in sword and shield.
David, too, was a shepherd and solid as a rock.
He told it like it was with his harp and his walk.
These humble shepherds were impressed that God did care,
So they went out in a rush to share the Glad News everywhere.
Once more we celebrate Christmas, my dear friend.
Will you go from the manger, a lost world's hunger to attend?
Though most don't know it is salvation they lack;
Spinning their wheels, their train is right off the track.
Buying and selling, getting and sending, having is the word.
Blind they are to Jesus – most have never heard.
So dear friend, go and make a difference – you are sent.
Go like the shepherds, sharing God's Good News, until you
are spent.

November 2000

Some People Say

Oh, that again! I've heard it all,
A Baby born in Bethlehem stall,
A young mother, almost a child,
Shepherds running from the fields, almost wild.

Songs in the air, even a chorus,
Singing of peace and goodwill for us.
Giving glory to God in the highest,
Born the Savior of all the mightiest.

"What's that you say, Lord? It's all for me?
But it's a new millennium, can't you see?
I'm too busy; I haven't time.
After all, it now seems to me like some mime."

But God's says "Listen! I have spoken.
This is my word; it's not a token.
What I've said in Jesus, my Son,
Is for every Tom and Sally, Pearl and Ron.

You're limited by the time that's for you,
But I'm eternal; I made time, that's true.
So get with it fast and stay in touch.
You celebrate Christmas 'cause I love you much!"

Speculation

While some folk are content to speculate,
We are glad that our God makes us sure.
He doesn't leave us alone to doubt and wonder;
He comes to us with love, holy and pure.

In the fullness of time, He comes as He will,
And He sends a little Baby to everyone – to you.
Born in a manger, young Mary's firstborn Son,
Jesus comes, God's love revealed, God's will to do.

Oh, men speculated, those who couldn't believe,
That God would come simply so all could know,
"Art thou He, or are we to look for another?"
Oh, He comes to a stable, there's a star, no great show.

Humble shepherds on a hillside hear an angelic chorus;
A messenger tells them to run to that special stable.
There they will find Him born and all wrapped up warm;
Mary and Joseph are amazed, and showing their caring as
they are able.

These were those who speculated, King and priests,
Also the lawyers and experts of God's Holy Writ,
"But this is not the way He is to come," they said.
Yet there He is, prophecy fulfilled every bit.

We can never ever do it by ourselves;
We can't figure out a way to save the world.
That's beyond our selfishness and our egotism;
Only God is able – He, who into space the planets hurled.

June 8, 1997

They Came! They Went!

A bright star up in the sky;
The wise men on camels slow,
Riding long by day and night;
Star led, they onward go.

The star, one night, stands right still;
The wise men found the child.
Each offered a special gift;
Mary's heart was beating wild.

The hours quickly pass away,
The wise men rise to go;
They now return by another route,
On their camels, tall and slow.

This Carpenter

Joseph was of a stubborn kind
He knew not the meaning of a "NO."
He looked until at last he found
A place for Mary, with a manger low.

How much he helped with the birth
Of the Son of God that night,
We do not know, but we can guess –
It was for him quite a sight.

Some things were surely new to him,
This carpenter of a holy, single mind.
The inner strength that bore him up
Was of a very special kind.

Like Him, may our date with destiny
Find us able to meet the test;
To do and be and say and think,
For Him, nothing but the very best.

December 1997

To Love and Adore

Son of God, born of Mary of Nazareth,
It is you we seek to love and adore.
Help us cast off all the excess baggage;
Too much display! All the trimmings galore!

Here are our hearts and lives –
We put them all into your hands.
Take us and use us to help others daily;
Your salvation, to reach and win all the lands.

You are the Evangelist par excellence;
Your interest and terms take in the whole world.
We may never really fathom all the great love
That you in Jesus displayed and fairly hurled.

December 17, 2005

Twinkle

Amid the Heavens, I, too, twinkled,
On that cold and silent night.
My Father's Son was aborning
As I shed my feeble light.

Not much was I, there a shining,
While God's plan was being fulfilled,
But what light I had inherited,
This I shared as it I spilled.

Far and wide I sped earthward,
Giving all I had to give,
To let you, too, my brethren,
Reflect His light as you live.

His beckon comes to us all;
He invites us ourselves to lose,
To join in the battle for the Kingdom,
Is our great privilege to choose.

Thus in this world where there is darkness,
We are asked to reflect His Eternal light.
Following in the footsteps of our Master,
We keep making His world more bright.

December 21, 2001

We Celebrate You, Lord

Jesus, what do You think by what You see,
In the way we humans celebrate Your birth?
Does it cause You to smile and laugh with glee,
Or does it sadden You with a joyless dearth?

'Tis true that many miss the reason;
They don't even realize that You came.
They can't grasp that this is Your season
And that You've come to leave nothing the same.

Your touch, Your presence, makes all things new;
You're no longer a baby in a cradle or a box,
You, the Child, the Healer, the Prophet and Preacher, too –
Your crucifixion, Your resurrection, blasts us out of our sox.

You're no "has-been" belonging to way back then;
You are our Emmanuel, You're always right here.
You don't belong to the ifs, the doubts, and the maybes,
When You're the conqueror of death, hell, and fear.

There's no one, there's nothing found anywhere,
That can begin to match what You've been and done;
Your presence and power, found right here and right there,
Includes us all, our hearts You've won.

We bow the knee; we worship You, Lord;
We sing Your praises on this Christmas Day.
We celebrate Your coming, the Living Word,
God's greatest gift of love, in a manger filled with hay.

June 2007

We Would Make Ready

We would make ready a lovely place;
Humble though it be, and most bare.
'Tis our hearts you hear joyfully beating;
We come to thank you for your care.

You come to us as you came of yore;
Heavenly chorus still fills our skies.
Our faith reaches to Bethlehem's cradle,
Daring to believe with gladsome eyes.

We need no plane, no ship, nor camel;
We, by faith, cross the distance on faithful wing.
We rejoice in our hearts for the Baby,
Jesus Christ, our destined Savior and King.

We would each day be more faithful;
We do follow where Thy feet have trod.
In Thy service we seek to witness,
Rejoicing, proclaiming our wondrous God.

When we can no longer proclaim Thee,
When it seems we be out of breath,
We look to thee for strength and mercy,
That in Thee we be faithful 'til death.

When Heaven's portals wide open beckon
Beyond the cradle, the cross, and open tomb,
We shall look to Thee while rejoicing;
Blessed Fruit Thou art, from Mary's womb.

We would rejoice where'er we be.
Thy Son, oh God, has come for all.
Through Thy love and for Thy caring,
That doth uplift us, should we fall.

December 6, 2003

Welcome To His Shed

From how far away had they come
Before they were refused at the inn?
Journey-worn, both man and beast,
Little impression made on the village din.

Care and rest was their greatest need;
And really time to be all alone.
"In the fullness of time," Oh, it's here!
Heaven would attest as the stars shone.

Though there was no other place,
There was the stable, a cave-like shed.
This would do for the Creator's Son
At home everywhere, He could lay his head.

Later, He would share with all,
The rich, the poor, the lost, the least;
His love, once given room in the heart,
Would grow and grow as Heavenly yeast.

"Thy kingdom come, Thy will be done,"
This is the theme He would teach.
God's kingdom, both without, within;
Faith brings salvation within reach.

Oh, what glory came that night!
What miracle happened in that shed!
Mary gave birth to little Jesus;
In a lowly manger, she laid His head.

It's never far to that shed.
Everyone is welcomed at the stall.
It just takes a silent, open heart
To give time to the Spirit's call.

Let's take time to pause, to listen.
We, too, can hear the angels sing.
Peace on earth, goodwill to men!
Glory to God, let the heavens ring!

December 24, 2000

What Hast Thou Done?

O God, my Lord, what have you done?
You've come to us; you've come with Love.
You've sent to us your own dear Child,
Whom we worship with hearts beating wild.

Never before had you come like this.
This, all this, signifies great eternal bliss.
Our faith now in your only Son sets us free;
No longer a slave to sin, now we really see.

Let us shout it aloud, my own dear brother.
God chose Mary to be His obedient mother.
She complied and here – Alive He Is!
Emmanuel, cradled in a manger, a Miracle it is!

Just keep us closer with you all the way,
We want to love and serve you every day.
This life, our life, belongs to you.
You have our faith, our loyalty, too.

2002

When He Came

While the doctors feverishly searched the sacred books,
The wise men glanced with doubting looks.
Why could not men like these well-bred
Know the answer? But, no instead.

Their fumbling attempts gave them away,
They knew not for sure His coming day.
There was the chance that in Bethlehem low
Was the place where they should really go.

So the wise men went with their hopes held high,
Following the star in the Eastern sky.
Once they were there, the star stood still;
Their hearts beat fast; it was God's will.

They came from afar with sure step and slow;
Now they worshiped Him as they bent low.
With gifts and songs of praise on their lips,
They turned for home on their desert's ships.

No crafty king would hear them talk!
They would go home by another walk.
Later, when all was safe and sure,
They could give their count in language pure.

In sin's dark world of fear and hate,
There oft is no one to open the gate.
God does with love what men cannot do,
And keeps the floods of salvation flowing through.

December 2004

Which Was Just As They Had Been Told

We are like two men on the way to Emmaus, after the resurrection;
About many of God's promises and His works, His miracles,
He is the only One! He is able!

The shepherds out among the hills
Were privileged on that night.
The heavenly chorus filled the skies,
And the angel appeared in dazzling light.

The chorus sang of peace and good will;
God was sending His best to earth.
"Go to Bethlehem and look for Him,"
The angle declared His place of birth.

"Let's go and see if this be true,
In a manger we're to find the Child."
Could it be that they heard well,
With hearts beating ever so wild?

Arriving there, "Lo, in a manger lay
The Baby wrapped in humble fare."
They shared their story, faces open and wide,
As Mary showed the Baby tender care.

So they shared and were amazed.
"Could He be the awaited, Promised One?"
One thing for sure, the shepherds knew,
It was just as the angel said it would be done.

Now, lo, these many years gone by,
We, too, speed as they also sped;
Our hearts beat wild within our breasts,
As to the manger we are led.

Oh, Little One, who became a Child,
And later still became a Man,
You love me, too, as You speak my name.
I come in faith as best I can.

You died for us upon that cross,
As God raised You from the tomb;
Eternal life You give to us,
Predestined Savior, from Mary's womb.

January 1999

Who Heard the Angels on That Night?

Who heard the angels on that night,
Singing in the heavens? Oh what a sight!
It was the shepherds who heard them sing,
Saying, "To all the world, Good News we bring!"

"Glory to God in the highest," if you will;
They came with the message of peace and good will.
They said "Go to Bethlehem! Go find the little Child!
He is God's messenger, holy and undefiled."

They said, "Go to Bethlehem and in a manger low,
You'll find Joseph and Mary, faces all aglow."
Did they go to Bethlehem as they were told?
Yes, they ran; and the night was really cold.

They shared what they had heard and seen.
Mary told her story; the shepherds' spirits were very keen.
How did the shepherds go when they went?
They left the Holy Family as ones called and sent.

They, with enthusiasm, told what they had seen and heard;
The promises fulfilled and bound in His Holy Word.
Who else came to visit Bethlehem in due time?
Kings from the East on camels came with gifts sublime.

Gold, frankincense and myrrh they did bring.
They honored and worshipped little Jesus, the King,
Who was born and destined to save us all.
Jesus is His name – the Remedy for the fall.

Manger and cradle, cruel cross and opened grave;
These tell the story how God came to save.
We read it, we believe it, we share it, too.
It tells us of Jesus, of Salvation for me and for you.

Willie's List

"I'm going to make my Christmas list." said Willie.
"No, it's not for what I want; it's my list for others, Silly."

Let's see, I'll want to get something for Mommy and Daddy,
And then I can't forget something for my dog called Laddie.

I suppose I gotta give a gift to Sister Susie – but not much.
She's my sister, but she bothered me, especially when I was on
that crutch.

Then some for Joey, my brother, but he's a mess.
He stole my wagon, hid it, and made me guess and guess.

Of course, I'll get a gift for my little baby brother.
He's so cute and really, I love him better than the other.

I've a good friend – he and I really are quite a pair.
We're great pals and we always do to each other what's fair.

I've got to dig deep in my savings for a gift for him.
I'll not be able to buy just any old thing on a whim.

But that new kid down the street that hit me in the eye,
I think I might work up some surprise to make him cry.

I can't forget my teacher; she even bragged on me a bit.
I'd bet she'll have trouble deciding where to let my little bell sit.

You know there's Johnny, who keeps getting me off key;
At the concert, Mr. Highnote even pointed directly at me.

I'll be blamed if I'm going to take anything over there,
And if I did, I'd get him a singing sour noted Teddy Bear.

I was listening to what the preacher was saying last week –
And come to think of it, I must turn the other cheek.

And he also said that God sent the baby Jesus, His Son,
Because He loves us in the night, and till day is done.

And you must love and forgive others for what they do,
'Cause if you don't, it's doubtful you'll be forgiven, too.

Maybe I had better take a second look at my list,
And decide to treat everybody better, and include those I've missed.

I'm sorry, God, that I didn't love them all.
Make me able to do better and stand up tall.

Wonderings

On the night when Christ was born
Of the blessed virgin called Mary,
Joseph came, leading a little friend.
The donkey had a precious load to carry.

Where did he rest and what did he eat?
What did he dream while fast asleep?
Did he know when the shepherds came,
Leaving one alone, the fold to keep?

Did there come also a shepherd boy,
Carrying a little lamb close to his heart?
Did he offer it with his loving care,
That stilled its bleating from the start?

After the long blessed vigil was over,
The sharing really began to start.
The shepherds and the Holy Family
Spoke freely from the heart.

These devout souls, with hearts ablaze,
Went back their flocks to keep.
But as they went, they shared with all –
The Good News, they could not keep.

May this Christmas do the same for us.
May God fill and bless our hearts.
May He take and use us as we go –
For from this hour, our mission starts.

December 1997

LaVergne, TN USA
12 May 2010
182529LV00004B/5/P